TALK YOUR WAY TO THE TOP

How to Address Any Audience Like Your Career Depends On It

Kevin Daley and Laura Daley-Caravella

McGraw-Hill

New York   Chicago   San Francisco   Lisbon   London   Madrid
Mexico City   Milan   New Delhi   San Juan   Seoul   Singapore
Sydney   Toronto

3 4 5 6 7 8 9 0   AGM/AGM   0 9 8 7 6 5 4 3

ISBN 0-07-140564-X

McGraw-Hill books are available at special quantity discounts to use as premiums and sales promotions, or for use in corporate training programs. For more information, please write to the Director of Special Sales, Professional Publishing, McGraw-Hill, Two Penn Plaza, New York, NY 10121-2298. Or contact your local bookstore.

This book is printed on recycled, acid-free paper containing a minimum of 50% recycled, de-inked fiber.

Library of Congress Cataloging-in-Publication Data

Daley, Kevin, 1931–
   Talk your way to the top / by Kevin R. Daley and Laura Daley-Caravella.
      p.   cm.
Includes bibliographical references and index.
   ISBN 0-07-140564-X   (hardcover : alk. paper)
   1. Business presentations.   2. Public speaking.   I. Daley-Caravella,
Laura.   II. Title.
   HF5718.22.D35   2003
   651.7'3—dc21
                                        2003006032

To those special people whose inspiration and insight helped make this book a reality:

Ann Goodson Daley   Elizabeth Lanza

David Caravella   Bob Daley

Acknowledgments

With special thanks to:

Our colleagues:

Charlie Windhorst	John Vautier
Jack Swanson	Jeanne Tingo
Kent Reilly	Henry Cohen
Eric Baron	Emmett Wolfe
Carol Samuel	Al Keiser

Our contributors of ideas, content, and graphics:

Charles Lanza	Lee Velta
Tom Hill	Alan Gilburne
Jim Kinnear	Jim McGuirk

Our publishers:

Jeffrey Krames   Ann Wildman

Our Content Wrangler:

Mia Amato

Contents

Introduction

BEFORE COFOUNDING COMMUNISPOND IN **1970** with my friend and business colleague, Charlie Windhorst, I was a management supervisor for the J. Walter Thompson (JWT) advertising agency. I was responsible for handling some advertising accounts at JWT, but, because of my interest and experience with presentations, I was also assigned to the new business development team.

I'll never forget my first experience pursuing a new account. Someone at JWT had heard a rumor that a certain big advertiser was unhappy with its agency—one of our big competitors. I was asked to call the president of that company and see if I could set up a meeting. I was told not to bring up the subject of a possible switch of agencies, but to give him the opportunity to do so. I was pretty confused by those instructions, but I made the call.

The president answered his own phone (miracles still happen), said, "Hello," and suddenly I had to say something. Here's what came out of my mouth: "Hello, my name is Kevin Daley, vice president of J. Walter Thompson. I was reviewing our records today and discovered that we have never established the right kind of relationship with you."

At that point I shut up; I didn't know what else to say anyway. His response was: "I don't know anything about the relationship you might have with someone here, but we are considering making a change in our agency set up and I'd like to talk to your management about whether or not J. Walter Thompson would be interested in soliciting our account."

Wow! I couldn't believe my good luck. The meeting took place and a date for a new business presentation was established. We knew we'd be up against four or five other top agencies—it would be a "bake off," a "beauty contest," a "dog-and-pony show."

Everything depended on the presentation.

We needed to highlight our talents, our creativity, our skills, our people, and our accomplishments. The presentation would be made up of many parts and involve several people. We started the planning process by creating an agenda and identifying the presenters. We notified all eleven presenters and told them what content they should emphasize. Finally, we scheduled two rehearsal times for each presenter. I rehearsed each of them personally. They hated rehearsing. They liked to talk about the material instead of delivering it. But that doesn't work. The words need to have traveled their route previously or they will take detours when they are launched to a live audience. The same is true for gestures and the handling of charts. Life is physical and so is presenting; we must physically go through the process to learn it. Then we must do it again (do it, not talk it) if we want to improve.

Were they good presenters? Some were. Most weren't. Were any of them great? No. They were experienced and competent, but not highly skilled. Some talked to their charts, not to the audience. Some mumbled or swallowed words. One senior vice president, whose name was Bill, read his script hidden behind a lectern while a cohort controlled his visuals. They leaned on the table; they slouched; they put their hands in their pockets. None of these things are punishable by death. But these people were the cream of the crop, the best that JWT had to offer. And yet they ranked good, not great, as presenters. This started me thinking: *There should be a training program for people whose livelihood depends upon making great presentations.*

When the big day arrived, the client showed up with his team and was taken to the main conference room, which had been designed as a mini theater for just this purpose. There was a conference table at floor level, with seats behind it.

The meeting began with eight client representatives and five JWT people seated around the table. Most of our presenters were on standby, outside the room. Our chairman opened, welcomed our guests, and established the agenda. In the dialogue that followed, the client identified why they were there and what they were looking for. Once that discussion was over, we began our presentation.

Our executive vice president started by giving a presentation on the subject, "Who is the J. Walter Thompson company?"

Next, individual case histories were presented on five accounts: Standard Brands, Kodak, Ford, Listerine, and Miles Laboratories. Five different account supervisors delivered these. They showed print ads and television commercials. They articulated marketing and creative strategies. They outlined budget efficiencies and return-on-investment. Our research director gave a presentation on copy testing; the media director, on media; the broadcast director, on broadcast. The creative director presented the creative philosophy of the agency. And our president handled the finale, showing a reel of JWT television commercials with his commentary.

When it was over, I thought to myself, "This could have been so much better." Our material was first class but, with a couple of exceptions, our presenters weren't. Imagine how much of a downer it was when Bill walked behind the lectern to read his presentation to the client. There was no lift, no charm, no sense of confidence.

In advertising lingo, we were "pitching for the account." Everything depended upon the client's reaction to the presentation. We could win a $50 million account if our presentation knocked the lights out. But, alas, the lights were still on when we finished. We didn't get the business.

I came to realize that, in the advertising business, decisions are made in response to an oral presentation, rather than a written proposal. (Later on I discovered that's true in virtually every business.) The proposal was important. It had to be there. The differentiator was the presentation, however. The client could see, hear, and sense what the recommendation was all about. They could ask questions. They could see the people who would be involved, assess their credibility, their commitment, their integrity, their enthusiasm, and their knowledge.

The presentation is a moment of truth for the presenter. We can't hide. We are exposed, for better or worse. The listeners decide whether they like us, believe us, trust us, and perceive whether we are secure in ourselves and confident in what we are saying. The viewers can see us think on the spot, and judge how smart we are.

In this moment, I had just witnessed the best efforts of the top people of the number-one advertising agency in the world and found them wanting. So I said to myself, "There is a need for a training company that helps successful people learn to present themselves better in front of an audience. They need it even more than people who are just starting out because so much is riding on how they handle themselves."

I founded Communispond because of that experience. Since then, the company has trained more than 450,000 executives in a broad variety of communications skills. And my passion in life continues to be helping people speak as well as they think.

In the pages that follow, my daughter Laura and I share the knowledge and findings that come from our collective forty-nine years of experience in training executives to be more effective in front of groups. Each chapter deals with a specific speaking situation you will face as you go forward. We explain what is expected of you and how to approach each one. We also provide a pathway for success in each of them. There are examples, stories, principles, and dos and don'ts for each situation.

Our goal in writing this book is to help you to be a more effective speaker, presenter, and communicator, no matter what challenges you may face. A by-product of this newly acquired skill is that you will also become a better leader, since leadership gravitates to people who can stand up and say it right.

1

AFRAID? YOU ARE NOT ALONE!

WHEN I WAS TWENTY-FIVE YEARS OLD, my father, Arthur Daley, won a Pulitzer Prize (see Figure 1-1). He was a sports columnist for the *New York Times*—the first ever to be so honored. I had just finished four years as a Navy jet pilot, flying off aircraft carriers and having the time of my life. Laura, my first child, was about to be born. I was scrambling around New York City trying to find a job so that I could make a living as a civilian and be able to support my family.

Figure 1-1. Photo courtesy of the authors.

I was impressed with my father, but not as much as I should have been. I didn't appreciate how great an honor the Pulitzer was. To me it was just another award, and he received lots of them. But as the days went by, people were constantly talking to me about it. How rare the accomplishment was. How he was the first in his profession. "Wow!!" they would say, "You must be so proud."

It began to sink in. I began to look at my father differently, more as a hero, of sorts, instead of the man who couldn't understand why I was having so much trouble finding a job. I began to realize that he was at the top of his profession. He was really something special. Everyone looked up to him and admired him.

A DINNER IN HIS HONOR

One day he said to me, "There is a dinner in my honor scheduled next Thursday night. Do you want to come?" "Who'll be there?" I asked. (No sense in my commenting on what an ungrateful question that was.) "Just about everybody in the sports business," he said.

So, on Thursday night, my father and I, along with fifteen hundred other attendees in full black-tie regalia, went to the Waldorf-Astoria to honor Arthur Daley, the first sports writer ever to win a Pulitzer Prize.

I was astonished at the number of people. The cocktail hour preceded the dinner and everyone talked sports, my favorite subject. And I was introduced as the son of Arthur. I couldn't have had better credentials; I was having a really good time.

THEY WANT ME TO SPEAK

Suddenly, Nat Goldstein, the special events manager for the *New York Times*, sidled up to me and said, "Kevin, we want you to be one of the speakers tonight. You will sit up on the dais and be the fourth speaker."
I was dumbstruck. It was like a bowling ball hit me in the stomach.
"I don't speak," I said.
"But this is your father who is being honored. You know him better than anybody here. It would be easy for you to speak for ten minutes or so and tell us about him from your viewpoint."
"You don't understand," I said. "I can't stand in front of an audience and speak. I avoid it at all costs. I'm not a speaker. Nothing will come out. I can't do it."

THE DIE IS CAST

"Well, Kevin, let me tell it the way it is," replied Goldstein. "You will sit on the dais. Your name is printed in the program. At a certain point you will be introduced as the next speaker. The audience will applaud. Then you can decide whether you will just sit there, or you will walk to the lectern and speak. There is nothing I can do about this. My job right now is to let the speakers know the order in which they will be called. Good luck to you; I know you can do it."
He walked away.
That was the end of the really good time I was having. I found my seat on the dais. The dais was a long table, raised up on a platform, with about twenty-five seats facing the audience. It was occupied by the most important people in attendance: the mayor, the governor, two senators, Cardinal Spellman, owners of the New York sports teams, and others.

DINNER IS SERVED

Gradually they all sat down and dinner was served. I, of course, sat there in terror. I scribbled a few notes, repeated my opening lines over and over, and tried to eat some of the dinner. I could chew but I couldn't swallow—no saliva. I washed a couple of chunks of food down with water and then gave up. This had turned into a nightmare, and my name hadn't even been called yet.

The main course was over. The master of ceremonies walked to the lectern and began. The first speaker was the mayor. The second was Jack Mara, co-owner of the New York Giants football team and my father's best friend. He was good and said nice things. I could see that my father was enjoying this. I don't remember who the third speaker was, just that I wished he would talk forever. He didn't—I heard myself introduced,

"And now ladies and gentlemen, Arthur Daley's son, Kevin."

MY TURN TO SPEAK

I somehow walked to the microphone. I still remember the stilted language of my opening phrase. (I memorized it then, and it has painfully run through my mind so many times since.)

"It is not for a junior member of the clan to extol the merits of its headmaster . . ."

I stumbled through ninety seconds and sat down. The audience applauded, of course. They always applaud. But I knew I had not done well. So did they. So did my father.

Others spoke, some with eloquence, some with humor. All were laudatory. Then my father spoke. He was funny and self-deprecating. They roared and cheered. Everyone seemed to be having a good time. Except me. I sat there wallowing in my failure. I had let my father down. I had the opportunity to make my father proud of me at the moment of his greatest triumph, and I didn't do it.

THE NEXT DAY

The next day I hugged my father and said I was sorry. He said, "You did all right. Most of them talked too long. You seemed to realize that shorter is better." I didn't buy that but was glad he said it. It demonstrated that you can always find something to praise if you try hard enough.

Within a day or so, I signed up to take the Dale Carnegie course, which is one of the best self-help programs for people afraid to stand up and speak in public. It was a tremendous help. It gave me confidence, and confidence is like a baby's first step. Everything else depends on it. I saw, by observing others in this program, that many people suffered from the same stage fright that I felt. Later, when I began to study the subject, I discovered that even some great men of history had stage fright, or experienced the same fear.

HOW UNIVERSAL IS THE FEAR?

Cicero, one of the great philosophers of the world, who lived in the first century B.C., wrote that all good public speaking was characterized by nervousness.

Benjamin Disraeli, known in England in the 1800s for his dramatic political views, once said that he would rather have led a cavalry charge than faced the House of Commons for the first time.

William Jennings Bryan, one of the great American orators of the twentieth century, admitted that, in his first attempts, "his knees fairly smote together."

More recently *The People's Almanack Book of Lists* printed the results of a survey of three thousand Americans. One of the most startling outcomes was the answer to the question: "What are you most afraid of?" The results appear in Figure 1-2:

What are you most afraid of?

Speaking before a group	41%
Heights	32%
Insects and bugs	22%
Financial problems	22%
Deep water	22%
Sickness	19%
Death	19%
Flying	18%

Figure 1-2. From *The People's Almanack Book of Lists* by David Wallechinsky, et al. Used by permission of Bantam Books.

A SURVEY—WHAT ARE YOU MOST AFRAID OF?

You can see from the percentages that this survey elicited more than one response per person.

But it's important to recognize that there were no multiple choices involved in this survey, no hints to lead the respondents. It's called an "unaided" survey. A cross-section of America searched its collective soul and 41 percent said, "Speaking before a group is what I fear most."

When the same question was asked on an "aided basis," which means the respondents are given a list of probable fears to select from, more than 90 percent selected speaking before a group.

FEELINGS OF NERVOUSNESS

So if you have ever felt the roaring wings of butterflies fluttering around in your stomach before a presentation, you are just like the rest of us, part of the Human Race. A dry mouth is normal. So is a feeling of tension. So is a quaver in your voice, a sense of awkwardness, not knowing what to do with your hands, shortness of breath, sweatiness, a somewhat sickly pallor, and more.

It's hard to pin down what causes this virtually universal fear. The simplest explanation is that when you stand up to speak to a group you see a superior force out there. *All those people.* And it's them against you. A primal safety valve flicks open. The central nervous system sends you an extra jolt of adrenaline to help you meet this challenge.

PART OF THE HUMAN CONDITION

It's the same adrenaline rush and the same question that your ancestors faced back in the Stone Age, when they suddenly came face-to-face with a saber-tooth tiger. Fight or flight? Do they stay there and fight or do they run for the hills? No matter what their decision, they needed all the adrenaline they could get.

I share this with you so that you will see that you are not alone if you suffer stage fright or fear of speaking in public. It happens to everyone. It's simply part of the human condition.

But let's stop here. We don't overcome fear by wishing it were gone. There is a process involved, and I don't want to gloss over it.

THE FIRST THREE STEPS IN OVERCOMING FEAR

Back in the early days of broadcasting, one of the great newsmen was Lowell Thomas. He would be equivalent today of Dan Rather or Tom

Brokaw. Thomas was a strong believer in the importance of being able to speak your mind in front of a group. One of his statements is particularly meaningful if you are concerned with improving your station in life. He said, "The speaker's platform is inevitable for the man on the way up."

His use of the word "man" is generic; his statement is meant to imply all of humanity. So let's approach it the way we would any inevitable human situation. Learn about it, decide what to do, and learn how to do it well.

STEP ONE—ADMIT YOUR FEAR
Admit to yourself that your fear of speaking in public is hurting you. It is limiting your opportunity for recognition and advancement. It is holding you back. It is embarrassing you. It has no advantages, only disadvantages.

STEP TWO—EXAMINE POSSIBLE SOLUTIONS
You and I are not unique. There are hundreds of thousands like us. Which means there are hundreds of programs available to you. Dale Carnegie is one, Communispond is another, Toastmasters is a third. Every adult education syllabus offers speaker training.

Some are better than others, of course, but any of them will help you. The most important criterion to look for is the number of "on your feet" speaking opportunities the program provides—the more the better. You don't overcome fear and develop self-confidence by listening to lectures.

Emerson said, "If you can do a thing once, you can do it twice. If you can do it twice, you can make a habit out of it." We learn by doing. Most of the skills that have to do with overcoming fear are physical, and we will discuss these types of techniques in Chapter 2.

STEP THREE—MAKE A DECISION
There's no sense wallowing around in all the material you may have uncovered. Select the course or training program that captures your fancy and sign up. If you are like me, you may have gotten this far many times in the past but procrastinated because the unknown is frightening.

But here is good news: The very act of making a decision will free you. The instant you make it you will feel good, perhaps even euphoric. That's one of the beautiful mysteries of life. Making a decision carries its own reward, independent of the work that will follow, perhaps because decisions are so difficult to make.

IT'S THE RIGHT THING

Tom Hill, a managing director at Communispond, tells about a time when he was driving from his home in Riverdale, New York, to Mount Holly, New Jersey, to teach a program the next morning. It was four o'clock on a Sunday afternoon and he had been on the road for two hours when it started to rain. He was only a half hour from the hotel, which was the next day's program site and where he would spend the night.

Suddenly, he wondered if he had put the class books and other necessary materials for the next day's program in the trunk. He stopped the car alongside the Jersey turnpike, opened the trunk, and—it was empty. The rain was pouring down, but that meant nothing to him. He was furious with himself. No way was he going to drive two hours home and another two hours back to be exactly where he was now.

He raged silently to himself. "Not fair. No way. I can do the program without the materials. The participants won't know the difference. I'll wing it. I've done enough of these to know what to do. I'll use magic markers. I'll make charts . . ."

Then he stopped and asked himself one question. What is the right thing to do? His answer was to turn around, drive back home, and get the materials. And that is what he decided to do.

Here is how he describes his feelings at that moment: "When I first realized my predicament, I was furious. I had been looking forward to getting to the hotel, having a relaxing dinner, and getting to bed early. Now I was churning inside. I was ready to tear my hair out.

"But once I faced up to my error and decided that I had to do what was right, I felt an amazing kind of peace settle over me. I had made my decision. So what if I had to drive an extra four hours, it wouldn't kill me. And, most important, I was pleased with myself because I was doing the right thing."

You will find the same kind of peace once you make a decision to take action. You won't have to wait. It will come upon you immediately. There will still be a lot of work to be done before you've accomplished your goals, but you will have begun. And you will be pleased with yourself.

KEY LEARNINGS FOR TAKING THE FIRST STEPS IN OVERCOMING YOUR FEAR

Do:

- Recognize that your fear of speaking is natural. You are not weird, you are normal.
- Admit to yourself that avoiding the speaker's platform diminishes you. You can't stand out in a competitive environment if you won't stand up and speak.
- Ask yourself, "What is the right thing to do?" Then take action and put the fear of speaking behind you.

Don't:

- "Put off till tomorrow." Take action today.
- Take solace in the thought that you are an introvert or a "behind-the-scenes person." That has nothing to do with being able to speak.
- Try to get out of it when the opportunity to speak presents itself.

HOW TO STAND UP
AND SPEAK AS WELL
AS YOU THINK

S
O NOW YOU'VE BEGUN THE PROCESS and have taken those steps outlined in the prior chapter. You're willing to face an audience but wouldn't refer to yourself as a pro. Then someone asks you to be a speaker at an upcoming event they are planning. Your first question springs up almost automatically: "What do you want me to talk about?" The answer is never really enough.

You will be given a subject and the setting will be explained, but that still leaves a lot of leeway in structuring your talk. You will be assigned a specific amount of time. Your role will be clear. But you will still have to prepare your talk, rehearse it, know it cold, and deliver it in front of a live audience. That involves a lot of work. Let's break the pieces apart and identify what you should do to give yourself the best advantage.

PREPARATION: MENTAL AND PHYSICAL

In its simplest form, preparation is having done enough work to be absolutely sure you know what you are talking about.

Abraham Lincoln once said, "I believe I shall never be old enough to speak without embarrassment—when I have nothing to say."

Churchill said it took him six or seven hours to prepare a forty-five minute speech. It's no walk in the park. If you want to be confident, you must know that your message is worthy of the audience, worthy of the moment, and worthy of you. That takes time and it takes work. And it is worth it. Your sense of triumph at the conclusion of your talk will come, in part, from knowing that you have worked hard for this moment.

KNOW YOUR SUBJECT

The first step in gaining confidence is to know your subject. There is no substitute for that. If you are not an expert on the subject, don't speak. You become an expert through study and experience. If you think about it, you may see that you are already qualified to speak on a number of subjects. Remember, someone else recognizes you as an expert and as a person who has experience worth sharing with a broader audience. That is why you have been asked to speak. But you still have to decide exactly what to say. The situation will usually determine the direction your remarks should take. For example, when I was asked to speak at the dinner for my father (Chapter 1), it was clear that I should have told a story that showed what a fine man he was and that I loved him.

KNOW YOUR AUDIENCE

When Lincoln spoke at Gettysburg, he knew his mission was to commemorate those who gave their lives on that battlefield site. He spoke briefly but was so memorable that not only the battle but the speech have become part of our common history. The president of the United States speaks to the country and to the world on the state of the union, the budget, the economy, foreign affairs, etc. The president also speaks in response to any significant happening that involves the United States. These public addresses don't ramble (thanks in part to an army of crafty political speechwriters) and are to the point.

A department head in a company speaks both internally and externally on the mission of the department, or about a special initiative, an unforeseen emergency, in recognition of someone's accomplishment, or to announce a promotion, for example.

You can see that events and your audience often determine what is expected of you. Your responsibility is to reach into your own storehouse of knowledge and experience, determine your point of view about the issue at hand, and then craft your message so it addresses the current need.

SHOULD YOU WRITE OUT THE TALK?
We live in an age where the computer is at our fingertips. We even use it to help us think. With that in mind, by all means, write out your talk. It will help you put your thoughts in order and your confidence will be buoyed by seeing the talk right there in front of you.

Then, read it over and over again. Read it out loud. Read it to your spouse, to a friend, to another family member, to your dog (if you can keep him sitting there, you know you are pretty good). *Read it in front of a mirror while trying to maintain eye contact with yourself as you read.*

Now you know the speech pretty well. Next, do the same talk without the script. Make notes if you like. Use them while you rehearse. On the day of your talk, you might even take the notes with you in your pocket to be used in an emergency, but leave the written script at home.

NEVER READ TO AN AUDIENCE
Never read a speech to an audience unless you are forced to do so. They deserve better and so do you. Think of your own experience. Have you ever been impressed when a speaker read a talk or a sermon to you? If your answer is, "No" (and I think it will be), then don't inflict the same pain on others.

We listeners are savvy folk. When a speaker begins a talk, the first thing we do is decide whether it's "live" (coming from inside the speaker's head) or it's "being read" (from a piece of paper on the lectern). They are not the same. "Being read" is "day-old bread." No matter how erudite the writing is, the audience sees the speaker as a reader of yesterday's news.

DID THE SPEAKER EVEN WRITE THE SPEECH?

An audience forced to listen to a speaker simply read notes may feel slighted or shortchanged. The drama is gone. We are not seeing the creation of a talk right before our eyes. We cannot even be sure the speaker wrote the speech. So we, fickle listeners that we are, will give the speaker demerits right off the bat.

But when a speaker begins a talk with head held high, looking at the audience as he speaks, we know that what we are hearing is "today's bread," baked fresh, right before our eyes. Our attention peaks. We are watching a live performance. We are impressed. The speech has hardly begun and we are awarding bonus points.

THE IMPACT OF THE AUDIENCE

You walk to the front of the room and turn to face the audience. There is that superior force out there, staring back at you. Every instinct says you should scan the audience. Your eyes almost wander by themselves. That's their job—to scan for news, to take the news value out of the room. Eighty-five percent of all information stored in the brain comes through our eyes. The eye is our primary sense. "Let me serve you," says the eye, "let me scan."

But scanning also exacerbates a feeling of nervousness. Your eye sends all that blurry audience information to your brain, and the brain doesn't know what to do with it all. So it throws up an emergency flag and signals for an adrenaline fix. You already have that gnawing tension in your stomach, knowing you are going to have to speak. Then you get that extra jolt of adrenaline to really jazz you up. Your nervousness is increased. Your thoughts get all jumbled. Your mind can even go blank. Whoa, Nelly!!

OUR INSTINCTS WORK AGAINST US

As speakers, what do we tend to do to combat all this? We slide into some pretty weak defensive behaviors:

- Looking away from the audience when searching for a word
- Looking at people without really seeing them
- Looking up, hoping for divine intervention
- Closing our eyes, briefly, when thinking
- Sweeping the room with our eyes

These are habits, or quirks. They are not personality traits. They are not an integral part of your psyche. You do them because you don't know what else to do. None of it helps you think better or speak better. And the impact on an audience is negative.

WHERE SHOULD YOU FOCUS?

Focus on one person, one pair of eyes. At Communispond, we call it "Eye-Brain Control." You remain focused on one person in the audience until you complete a thought. A thought is not a paragraph, it's a sentence or a phrase. It's a place in your dialogue where you might naturally pause. Usually it's more than five seconds but not as much as fifteen seconds in length. Then you move to another pair of eyes and complete another thought. You repeat the process over and over until you finish.

Does it work? Yes it does—better than any other remedy. Forget tranquilizers, alcohol, or hypnosis. The principle is simple, as are most great discoveries. When you focus on one person, you are reducing the audience to one individual. Your brain can handle that quite easily. Then you move to another individual. The situation becomes the same as what you face every day. You are used to speaking to one person at a time. You are good at it.

EYE-BRAIN CONTROL—THE NATURAL WAY

It's so natural when you think of it. The eye can't focus on more than one person at a time anyway. When you look at your boss, you can't simultaneously look at his or her assistant. The second person goes out of focus. By using Eye-Brain Control, you are back to doing what you do best—talking one-to-one.

Benefits of this technique:

- Gives you a way to control your nervousness
- Helps you read your audience by seeing the reaction of individuals

- Enables you to think better on your feet
- Helps you control your rate of speech
- Provides a way to cut back on non-words ("um, er," etc.)

WHAT ADRENALINE DOES TO OUR BODIES

The eyes are only part of the solution, in cooperating with the great adrenaline rush we get when we stand in front of an audience. Our bodies are super-charged too. It's more energy than we are used to. If we don't know what to do with it, this physical energy can work to our disadvantage. It sort of leaks out all over the place. We fidget, clear our throats, put our hands in our pockets, move our feet from side to side, scratch our heads, play with a pencil, run an index finger across our noses, and cross our feet, among other things.

None of that helps. But the energy will have its way. You've got to do something. You can't store energy. You've got to use it or it uses you. So what do you do?

WHAT TO DO WITH THE ENERGY

The answer is to use your body to add a visual dimension to the content of your talk. Gesture for emphasis. Gesture for excitement. Show physically that you believe and are committed to what you are saying. Increase your volume to add inflection and vocal emphasis to your message. That way, you use the energy productively. Let's examine this whole concept further.

Speaking to a group in its simplest form is . . .
Energy released (by the speaker) = Energy received (by the audience)

If we speak with low energy, the audience receives low energy, and our impact is reduced accordingly.

HOW A SPEAKER IMPACTS AN AUDIENCE

A few years ago a famous UCLA professor, Albert Mehrabian, conducted extensive research on the communications process. The chart in Figure 2-1 is drawn from those studies.

Impact of Communication

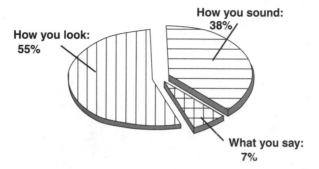

Figure 2-1. The Visual Impact of Communications. Adapted from *Nonverbal Communication*, © 1972 Albert Mehrabian.

What this chart shows is the relative impact of three factors when you speak to a group. How you look accounts for a whopping 55 percent. How you sound, 38 percent. What you actually say only accounts for 7 percent of the total impression you've made.

How you look includes your clothes, your facial expression, your stance, the leaning of your body, your hands, the way you move your eyes.

How you sound depends more on volume and inflection than the quality of your voice. Again, it's an impression.

Your words? Suppose you're trying to motivate a group of people and you tell them that something is "a great opportunity," but you don't look and sound it. They believe their eyes and ears, not your words.

HOW YOU LOOK
Let's examine some of the "how you look" mannerisms that can work against you when you face an audience (see Figure 2-2). Most of these are a result of trying to hold back and bottle up the adrenaline, the nervous energy that has been pumped into you to help you meet the challenge.

FIVE WAYS TO LOSE VISUAL IMPACT

Figure No. 1: Hands in pockets tries to create a casual impression. This can have the opposite effect of making you look

Figure 2-2. Don't lose 55% of your impact.

nervous. Also, it adds no plus value to your talk. And who said casual was a good way to look in front of an audience? You are much better off looking committed to what you are saying.

Figure No. 2: Guaranteed, if your hands twitch, opening and closing, everyone will notice. Don't forget, their eyes are scanning for news, too.

Figure No. 3: In this one, Velcro grabs your elbows and won't let loose. Your arms can't be fully extended because your elbows are stuck to your rib cage. You'll never be able to show how high is high or how wide is wide. Your gestures will be smaller, less interesting, and repetitious.

Figure No. 4: Some people say they like to move around. Imagine someone coming into your office and dancing around as they talk to you. Moving around only makes sense when you are changing location for a purpose.

Figure No. 5: In this picture the speaker has all the weight on one leg. Your energy is stuck, and your body knows it. If you tilt one way to release it, the audience wonders which way you will tilt next.

All of this nervous energy is leaking out; it is not helping you as a speaker. It is taking a slice out of the 55 percent segment (the "how you look" portion) of your impact.

WHAT TO DO WITH YOUR HANDS

Where should your hands be? When you begin, they should hang naturally by your side. Then they should be used to describe and emphasize what you are saying. Ideally, you should gesture with one hand at a time. If you use both together, they will tend to work in parallel, cutting the air up and down as you talk. This is called indicative gesturing, which is repetitious and adds some, but not a great deal, of value.

When you are able to use one hand at a time, your hand and arm movements can be descriptive as well as emphatic. From an audience viewpoint, this provides an almost infinite variety of visual stimulus that increases your impact and helps reinforce your message.

Remember, the audience is looking with their eyes even more than they are listening with their ears. They want something to happen up there. You, as a speaker, must encourage their eyes to focus on you, if you are going to hold their attention. Otherwise their eyes will drift somewhere else. And wherever their eyes go, their minds will follow.

WHAT ABOUT STANCE?

Somewhere in your mind you may have a picture of a speaker pacing back and forth while mesmerizing the audience. Maybe it's the fictional Elmer Gantry or the very real Vince Lombardi. But it's a mental image that makes us think that pacing while talking is a plus. It isn't. Walking around is of no value to the audience unless you are going someplace. Pacing is going noplace.

You look strongest and in greatest control when you plant your two feet shoulder-width apart, weight equally balanced, square to the audience. That way, all of your energy manifests itself in gestures, facial expression, and upper body movements. Your message is reinforced and made clearer by your physical behavior. Your confidence will grow as you sense the control.

A popular misconception is that women should do it differently, with feet close together or with one foot placed slightly behind the other. Not so. These postures rob the speaker of the authority she wants to convey.

THE IMPACT OF YOUR VOICE

If your volume is low, you are probably speaking in a monotone. If you are monotone you are boring (see Figure 2-3).

Figure 2-3. Don't lose 38% of your impact.

In the thirty-three years of Communispond's existence, we have trained more than 450,000 executives. Most of them, almost all, actually, don't speak with enough volume. The sound is too soft. This is true for females as well as males, upper level as well as lower level, all industries, professions, and the arts. You name it. Speakers think they are loud, but audiences don't. They think speakers are boring. They want more excitement, and volume is a big part of that.

LOW VOLUME, LOW INTEREST
Audiences read low volume as low conviction or low interest on the part of the speaker. Then they take a small mental jump and say to themselves, "If the speaker isn't interested, I'm not either." At that point you've lost them. Good-night, Irene.

Harry Holiday, the former CEO of Armco Steel, once said, "I think the greatest sin in business life is to be boring." Some people might argue with that, but I found it to be most insightful, as it pertains to public speaking. The greatest sin a speaker can commit is to be boring, because that loses the audience. Yet we see it all the time. Low volume is the greatest cause.

SHOULD YOU EXAGGERATE VOLUME?
You may be thinking, "What are you suggesting—that I go up there and shout?" We're tempted to say, "yes," just to get the point across. But, then you'd say, "This is crazy," and stop reading.

All speakers think they speak louder than they do. That's only because they are hearing themselves through the bone structure of their head as well as through their ears. And many people have been taught that they should speak in a conversational tone. Unfortunately, that doesn't work when you are speaking to an audience. You will be trying to contain the adrenaline, to hold back the energy, instead of letting go and using it. You'll swallow your words. Your body will be a reflection of your weak voice. You'll be conscious of your nervousness. No good.

A LEAP OF FAITH

But if you take a leap of faith and let your voice ring out, you'll find that your body will follow and your confidence will soar. You see, volume is a trigger mechanism. Once you push yourself hard for more volume, your body will say to itself, "Hey, wait a second. I'm just hanging out here not doing anything. Maybe I should dive into the fray and help get the message across."

Whammo!! Then you'll gesture, you'll emphasize more, your hands will beat the air, your face will contort a little bit to show feeling, you'll smile, you'll frown, you'll knit your brow, you'll smash one hand into another. Your voice will have character and timbre. Your speech will have passion. The audience will love it. And they will love you.

All of that will make you free. Free of fear, free of self-consciousness, and free of self-doubt. You will have taken all of that adrenaline, all that energy, and put it to work for you. Once you can do that, you will have found the "open sesame" to self-confidence when you speak in front of a room. *Always remember: Your volume is the best physical trigger, the key to making it all happen.*

MAKING THE MOST OF YOUR WORDS

As Mehrabian notes, the actual words you speak will usually account for only 7 percent of what the audience will grasp from a presentation. But when you're speaking on the spot, and you've got to say it right, every word must count.

THE FIVE FORMS OF EVIDENCE

To speak successfully, you must provide some evidence to support or back up your viewpoint or your recommendation. It's the evidence that makes what you have to say interesting and believable. It's the evidence that makes the presentation persuasive and memorable. Let's look at the forms of evidence as they can be used for a talk. There are five of them, and they are easy to remember because when you put the first letters together it spells PAJES (an obvious misspelling of PAGES, but still a good mnemonic):

Personal Experience (The Story)

Analogy

Judgment of Experts

Examples

Statistics/Facts

Let's take the last one first. It's where many speakers concentrate, but it's not the best tool—it's just the easiest and most familiar. Most of us use Statistics and Facts really well. We are taught that's what business is all about.

But that's not what people are all about. They're about flesh and blood and feelings. Statistics and Facts aren't, but the other kinds of evidence are. Those are the tools to call upon if you want to get inside the minds and hearts of your listeners.

We'll tackle Personal Experience (the story) in depth in Chapter 4 and again in Chapter 16. Let's look at the other four, as they are applicable to nearly every situation.

Analogy is a form of evidence that is often neglected because it takes a little more work and more than a little creativity to come up with a good one. Yet a good analogy can have real power when used properly.

Let's define it: An analogy is a point of similarity between two unlike things. The one we are most familiar with is the "tip-of-the-iceberg" analogy. This implies a warning: It's about seeing only a small portion of something and missing the significance of the whole.

All good analogies are visual and allow you to exaggerate a point without offending the listener's intelligence. Analogies bite into a listener's consciousness. They register and they stay there.

Judgment of Experts is simply a supportive statement by a person the audience would recognize as an authority. You must explain the expert's credentials if they are not known to your listeners. For best results the quotes of another person should be kept short. Visualizing the quotes on projected slides will increase the power of the quote in supporting your presentation.

An Example is a specific situation with various key factors similar to those of your premise. Examples are persuasive to the degree the audience sees them as paralleling his or her own situation.

Statistics and Facts have their place, of course—especially if they are astounding enough to wake up the crowd.

Visualizing your evidence, whatever the form, will increase the power it has in supporting your presentation.

THE IMPACT OF AN ANALOGY

Analogies can have amazing impact in any talk, in part because everyone understands them. Let's look at an example of that impact. First, some background. A few years ago, Charlie Windhorst was chairman of Communispond, and Jo Wein was the company's top sales producer. Jo was also as bright and competent a person as you could ever hope to have on your team.

Charlie had an important administrative project that had to be thought through and a plan developed. Jo, because of her variety of talents, was the ideal person to do the job and do it well. So he called her in one day, laid out the project, and asked her to take it on.

Now, let's look at it from Jo's perspective. Jo was juggling the needs and demands of five clients and was about to land another one. She was on a roll as a salesperson and, given the time, could double the business she already had.

Jo listened attentively, asked questions, and agreed it was important. Then she said, "Charlie, are you sure I'm the best person to handle the project?" Naturally, Charlie assured her that she was and then said, "But Jo, I'm curious, why do you ask?"

Jo said, "Charlie, I see the importance of the project. There's no question that it has to be done and done well. And I'm flattered that you would ask me to handle it. But Charlie, I'm handling over a million dollars' worth of business right now, and I have that much more in new business just inches away, if I can get to it.

"If I take on the project you outlined, it would take half my time for two months, and I wouldn't be able to get to the new business at all."

Charlie expected this push back, so he said, "Jo, I admire you for what you are doing on the sales front, but we need this project done and you are the best person for the job."

Jo could see she wasn't getting anyplace, so she used an analogy. "Charlie," she said, "don't you see what you would be doing? Asking me to take on that project would be forcing me to cut back on my selling. It's like taking your best racehorse and putting a two hundred pound jockey on her back."

CHARLIE'S REACTION TO THE ANALOGY

Charlie said afterward, "The racehorse analogy was so clear and so obviously valid that I agreed with Jo. I was resisting her arguments at first because I expected them, but we're in a sales race in this company, and I didn't want to slow down my best horse in that race."

Notice the mental picture Charlie carried away from that exchange. All new learning needs to find a way to connect to existing knowledge in order for it to be stored and retrieved for later use. That's one of the beauties of analogies. They make an easy connection to the audience's memory bank. And your listeners can play them back afterward, if necessary.

KEY LEARNINGS FOR SPEAKING AS WELL AS YOU THINK

Do:

- Seek an opportunity to speak. Ralph Waldo Emerson said, "Do the thing you fear to do and the death of that fear is certain."

- Prepare your talk, outline it, write it out, make notes, and wallow in the material. Rehearse it aloud until you are sick of it. Then go through it one more time.

- Focus on one pair of eyes at a time when delivering your speech. Your butterflies will fly away.

- Be physically dynamic. Use hands, gestures, and body to make your talk come alive. Your nervous energy will work for you, and you will soar.

- Use analogies to support the points you are making. People remember vivid mental images longer than they remember words.
- Speak up. Speak out. Speak loudly.

Don't:

- Try to hold back or be reserved as a speaker. The maggots of nervousness feed on that, and they'll eat you alive.
- Bring your hands together. Once you do, they'll establish a relationship and work in parallel. You need them operating one at a time to create excitement.
- Think you can solve nervousness by reading your talk. It takes a lot of training and experience to do that well. And the audience doesn't like it when you do.

3

HOW TO PRESENT UP THE MANAGEMENT CHAIN

MY CLIENT, PETER, IS A MIDDLE MANAGER who works for a giant telecommunications company. At his level, managers are required to update the executive vice presidents, two levels up the management chain, once every quarter. This is a good management practice because it gives middle managers exposure to senior management. It also keeps senior management informed via a voice that is closer to the customer.

Here was Peter's moment—an opportunity to shine in front of senior management—during a quarterly update. And it was unquestionably a memorable experience, though not the kind Peter wanted to remember!

THE PRESENTATION

Peter stood at the head of a large oval table with about thirty people around it. The four senior managers were on either side of him. Peter's presentation was first. He put up his first slide and began. All the executive vice presidents (EVPs) seemed to be paying attention—for the first few minutes. Then, out of the corner of one eye, Peter noticed something that made it hard for him to concentrate on what he was saying. One of the EVPs started to fidget with his Palm Pilot. Peter looked at the others around the table. They were still looking at him. Phew. Another minute passed, and Peter noticed that the attention of the senior managers had changed. Most of them were now watching the EVP with the Palm Pilot! Peter struggled. He looked at his slides to try and refocus. The EVP was still fidgeting.

THE EVP LEAVES THE ROOM

Then it got worse. The EVP with the Palm Pilot stood up as though he had received a signal to do so, turned, and walked out of the room. Yes, he walked out of the meeting after only five minutes! Peter was flabbergasted, as were his peer presenters who were, of course, desperately trying to figure out how to avoid the same fate!

The EVP's reaction was only different from many others because he physically exited the room. We have all been at meetings where senior managers were present in body only. Their minds were elsewhere, but we smiled at them and talked to them, and everyone in the room kept up the pretense.

LESSON LEARNED

In many ways the EVP was doing these middle managers a great favor. He taught them a business lesson that could last their careers (assuming they didn't all quit and join the Peace Corps!). We are notoriously a society of bad listeners. Our managers are also. To keep people in the room, we need to give them a reason to pay attention to our presentations.

KEY PREPARATION QUESTIONS

To enhance your credibility and avoid Peter's fate, here are some questions to consider as you prepare—specifically—to present up the management chain.

---

1. How can you get listeners interested and on track in the first thirty seconds of your presentation?
2. How long do you have for the presentation?
3. What kind of visual support will you need?
4. Where will you be giving the presentation?
5. Who will be in your audience?

Let us take the questions one at a time and see how we can build a presentation that stimulates management's interest and captures their attention.

1. How can you get listeners on track and interested in the first thirty seconds of the presentation?
Answer this question first: Why are you speaking to these senior managers? What will they gain as a result of listening to you for ten minutes or so? Kevin Weiss, president of Pitney Bowes Global Mailing systems, put it this way: "At my level, I can't be an expert on everything. I must rely on and trust the presenter to be that. In fact, I am an expert on nothing.

"I rely on my managers to know the facts and be conversant with the detail. The number one question I have is, what is the objective of this meeting and what decisions have to be made?"

To Kevin Weiss, and other senior managers, you start to demonstrate your credibility (or lack of it) right up front by giving them reasons you are worth listening to.

STATE THE PURPOSE

Start the meeting with a statement of purpose. Follow up quickly with an agenda that outlines the track you will follow. After the small talk and social amenities, begin the business meeting with this statement:

The purpose of this meeting is to . . .

Here are some examples of what your statement of purpose in your presentation might sound like:

"I'm going to update you on the unprecedented results of our marketing campaign and ask you to make some decisions about what we should do next."

"I hope to get your approval for a two-million-dollar investment in technology that I believe will get us a three-million-dollar return within the first two years of the expenditure."

"I will explain what caused our dramatic increase in revenue this month and why we think that positive trend will continue."

"I'm here to 'fess up' to our mistakes and share our plan for improvement."

In each of these examples, you'll notice how there are certain words that cause the ears to perk up. These words give the audience a reason for listening—words like "unprecedented," "fess-up," and "dramatic increase."

WHY SHOULD THEY CARE?
One of the best pieces of advice I ever got was from my friend Eric Baron, who also happens to be my old boss and a wonderful speaker. He said, "Whenever you are presenting to people, the first question you need to answer is, 'So What?' Why should the audience care about what you say?"

By headlining your presentations with a statement that answers the question "So what?" you are teaching your senior manager how to listen to you. You are also answering Kevin Weiss's first question, "What is the objective of this presentation and what decisions have to be made?"

2. How long do you have for the presentation?
My hope is that you are never expected to talk for more than fifteen minutes, with another five to ten minutes for questions. Although we are talking about presenting to senior managers, they are also human beings, and human beings have limited attention spans. Assume everyone in your audience has attention deficit disorder and lean

toward a shorter presentation rather than a longer one. No one has ever gotten fired for saving a senior manager some time.

3. What kind of visual support will you need?
As mentioned in the last chapter, research says that 85 percent of all information stored in the human brain comes through the eye. The eye is our primary sense. Its function is to scan for news. What kind of news? Any kind. If a mouse ran across the floor, where would your eye go? To the mouse, right? And so would the eye of everyone in your audience. Not 90 percent or 99 percent but 100 percent of sighted humanity would react the same way. It's the way we are made.

So why not use this piece of information to your advantage? Accept the fact that if you are making a presentation and there is nothing visually interesting up there, the eyes of the audience will wander. And when the eye wanders, so does the brain. But you can take advantage of this idiosyncrasy of senior managers and the rest of humanity by jazzing up your presentation with interesting visuals. Feed the eye of your listeners and you feed their brains. They will be impressed with you and your presentation.

The kind of visuals you will use will depend on what you have available to you and the size of your audience. Software such as PowerPoint can be very helpful to put information into graph and chart form, which will help the listener conceptualize, and therefore remember, the points you make.

Use a projector. Do this even with an audience of one, because if your visuals are bigger than life, *you* become bigger than life.

YOU ARE THE MOST IMPORTANT VISUAL!
If possible, stand while you give your presentation. When you do, there is more of you to see, which is automatically more visually stimulating and more memorable. You will also speak louder if you stand. And louder is better. Three out of four presenters speak too softly. When volume is down, the excitement is down. When excitement is down, you and your presentation become less interesting. And less interesting is a synonym for forgettable!

If you are in a large room where you are forced to be fifteen to twenty feet away from the audience, use a lavaliere mike—the kind that loops around your collar or tacks to your lapel and leaves your hands free. Don't ever risk your listeners saying, "Speak up!" or "We can't hear you!" Your words are fragile instruments that need the power of your voice and your energy in order to come alive.

DON'T EXPECT MIRACLES FROM A MICROPHONE

Only you can bring passion to your presentation. Don't expect the microphone to make you more interesting. It won't. As a matter of fact, don't expect the mike to perform any magic at all. It will make you louder. Period. If you are dull, a microphone enlarges the dull. If you are passionate, a mike will enlarge the passion.

You must speak as forcefully with a mike as without one. The forcefulness of your voice colors the language you use and gives it greater meaning. The greater the volume (within a reasonable boundary of course), the greater the intonation, the greater the inflection, and the greater the nuances you will be able to convey.

DRESS THE PART

If your office dress is business casual, make sure you err on the side of business versus casual. This gives the impression that you are more serious and committed to your work. As my grandmother used to say to my father when he was an adolescent, "Son, you need to make sure your clothes are clean and pressed when you go to work. Other people can't see inside you, as I can, to know how beautiful and smart you really are."

For the most part, senior management can't see inside us to see how beautiful and smart we are either. They need to see us demonstrate it on the outside. So let's look at the tools we have to use. In Chapter 2, we talked about voice, dress, and stance. Our two other tools are the visual words we use and the actual visual images that support our presentation.

USE VISUAL WORDS AND PHRASES IN YOUR PRESENTATION

One of my favorite bumper stickers says, "Visualize whirled peas." I love it. It asks you to put in a picture something that one would rarely think about: little green round things whirling around in a kind of cyclone effect.

That is only half the picture. The other half is much harder to visualize: world peace. Yet every one of us can come up with some picture of how we might represent that concept.

The bumper sticker works. It causes us to change words into a picture, a concept. We remember concepts, and therefore I remember that bumper sticker.

USE VISUAL AIDS

Use analogies, charts, and pictures with word messages under them. Use three colors on your visuals. There are three things that attract the eye: *action, color,* and *exaggeration.* You can remember those three with the acronym *ACE.* Your body is the *action*, the visual has the *color,* and your vocal emphasis and gestures are the *exaggeration.* Those elements are powerful tools. Use them to make your talk interesting and compelling.

4. Where will you be giving your presentation?
Location, location, location. You've heard that from realtors, now you'll hear it as it relates to a presentation. The location makes a difference. If you can adjust the location where you will be doing the presentation, you want a room:

• Where you can be the center of attention when presenting.

• Where your presentation will not be cramped. No tripping over wires. No crowding.

• Where the senior managers will be away from their offices. The best room is in neutral space, which makes the meeting feel more important to them.

• Where you have access to technical assistance in the unlikely event that you need help with the microphone, computer, or projector. (You hope it is unlikely!)

If you are setting up the meeting, by all means do it on home turf or turf that makes you comfortable. If the location helps increase your self-confidence, it'll show through in your presentation. It also reduces the chances the senior manager will be distracted by phone messages or personal interruptions.

5. Who will be in the audience?
Make sure you are very clear on why each of the attendees is there. If you are not sure, ask beforehand. You want to fulfill each person's

needs and expectations and you can't accomplish that without knowing who will be there and why. It sometimes happens that senior managers invite juniors from their departments in order to increase their
exposure and experience.

You have every right to know who is going to attend so that you
can personalize your presentation, as necessary, and greet these people warmly when they arrive.

FORMATTING YOUR PRESENTATION

Your presentation up the management chain will most likely have one
or more of the following purposes: to exchange information, suggest
action to be taken based on the information, or to get approval. The
viewpoint format will help you organize your presentation to work
best for the listener. Your goal, no matter what the subject, should be
to ask for action.

Knowledge is not power until it is turned into action.
—Aristotle

It's not the knowledge but the action that creates the power. Let's look
at an example most of us can relate to. Ask a group of twenty people,
"By a show of hands, how many of you are heavier than you want to
be and would like to lose weight?" The statistics say 85 percent of
those people (sixteen or seventeen of the twenty) will raise their
hands. Yes, they would like to lose weight.

Now ask, "How many of you feel you have the knowledge—you
know what you must do to lose weight?" Of that group, nine out of ten
will say that they know what to do.

ONLY ACTION HAS VALUE

Then ask the clincher question. "How many of you are doing it—doing
what it takes to lose weight?" You'll see only a few hands raised. So we
can kick ourselves all we want for being human, but the facts are all
around us. Knowledge doesn't do much good until action takes place.

How does this relate to a presentation up the management chain?
Often we will be presenting the latest findings, as well as a viewpoint
on a project, called a talk to inform. Theoretically, only the information is important. But is that so? Is our job over when we lay out the
information? Or is it incumbent on us to suggest an action, a next step?

If we put ourselves in management's shoes the answer is easy. We are the experts or we wouldn't be presenting to this august body. And if we are the experts, we should have a suggestion or recommendation as to what action is required. In reality, that is the conclusion to the presentation. If we leave it out we haven't given them their money's worth.

Information alone does nothing for you and it does nothing for them. Senior management will be waiting to hear what that information means to the organization and what action needs to be taken as a result. So bring it full circle. Suggest action or recommend the next steps that should be taken.

THE VIEWPOINT PRESENTATION FORMAT

1. Subject/Background

2. Viewpoint

3. Importance

4. Evidence

5. Summary of Viewpoint and Importance

6. Action or Next Steps

7. Questions and Discussion

Here is how to structure a viewpoint presentation. The format is organized on a logical basis and is consistent with how people listen best.

1. Subject/Background
This is what you are going to be talking about. State it clearly and succinctly so that everyone is on the same page. Your subject could be an issue or a concern that surrounds a policy, practice, or belief that is disputed or challenged. It should take less than a minute of your presentation time to present your subject. If you are using visual aids, the subject should have its own visual. By way of example, let's say the subject is: "A report about the declining service level this past month in our phone service unit, and our plans for improving it."

The Background is past information that helps put what you are saying into perspective. If last month you changed the scheduling of your phone service reps to better accommodate call volume changes, you might also remind your audience why you did that, what the existing service levels were, and what the call volume was. The background provides context that will help your listener interpret the new information you are about to give them. This would also have a separate visual.

2. Viewpoint

The Viewpoint is a one-sentence statement of your point-of-view on the subject. In the phone center example, the viewpoint might be that, "I believe we can reduce turnover and therefore increase service levels by hiring additional workers for the hours between 4 P.M. and 10 P.M., which is our high volume time period."

3. Importance

The Importance supports your Viewpoint and relates directly to timing. State how your Viewpoint improves the audience's understanding of the issue, as it exists now. Also state how that understanding can enable the company to act in a beneficial way. In our phone center example, this might be projections for reduced staff turnover, increased service levels, and money saved as a result of the reduction in turnover.

4. Evidence

Evidence builds credibility. Your Evidence should show that your Viewpoint is based on a solid understanding of the issue. You demonstrate that your Viewpoint is fair, takes into account the facts, is beneficial to society, and so on. Here is where we might use statistics or an analogy that supports our Viewpoint, or give examples of what success might look like. Use graphs, analogies, even photographs. The purpose of all Evidence is to help dramatize the correctness of your Viewpoint.

5. Summary of Viewpoint and Importance

The Summary should be simple and short. You are not repleading your case. You are merely restating your premise so that the picture is clear. It reinforces the essential story line of the presentation just before you introduce the action step.

6. Action or Next Steps

Here is where you ask for the commitment you need from the senior managers or state the Next Steps that you feel are indicated. In some cases it might simply be gaining concurrence or consensus. But usually what you will be asking for is formal approval authorizing you to move forward.

In the call center example, you would want agreement by the senior managers that the company could, indeed, reduce turnover and increase service levels by hiring additional people for the high volume 4:00 P.M. to 10:00 P.M. period. You would then ask for authorization to set that plan in motion.

7. Questions and Discussion

Be sure to include discussion time. You want reactions. You want questions. You need your senior managers' involvement. Obviously, you need authorization to go further, too, and it will never happen as a result of the presentation alone. The question-and-answer (Q&A) session is where senior managers get their arms around the subject. They test you with questions—some easy, some challenging. Here's where preparation pays dividends. Spend some time with your cohorts beforehand, predicting what questions might be raised and how you might handle them. Bring supporting material if indicated. You are the expert, so have your facts available.

Ultimately they will agree to go forward because of these factors:

* They buy your presentation and the case you make for proceeding in the new direction.
* They are impressed with *you*. They value your expertise and feel you are in control of the project.
* They have an overall sense of confidence that the project will succeed.

KEY LEARNINGS FOR PRESENTING UP THE MANAGEMENT CHAIN

Do:

* Refine and hone your presentation so it's on target, clear, and interesting. Keep it short. Ten minutes. Long will kill you; short will bring applause.
* Rehearse out loud, standing up, five times, all the way through. It will assure success. And you'll be proud of yourself besides.

- Make your visuals interesting. Get help. Bullet points and PowerPoint slides made up entirely of text won't do it. They're boring. Use pictures where possible.

- Know your content cold. If you drop the ball when challenged, you're dead. Your credibility will evaporate.

Don't:

- Start slowly with the thought that you'll pick up the pace later. This never happens! If you lose your listeners early, you won't get them back.

- Hand out copies of your slides beforehand or your listeners will concentrate on those instead of on you during your presentation. You don't need the competition.

- Stray from your prepared talk. If interrupted, ask your audience to write down their questions as they come up so you can address them at the end.

- Talk too much. Instead, surprise your listeners with succinctness, not length.

4

HOW TO BE
A LUNCHEON SPEAKER

IN CHAPTER 6, WE DISCUSS THE BUSINESS LUNCH as it can work one-on-one. What about when you are invited to address a business or professional luncheon group? Asked to share your words of wisdom? Give a lift to the group? Can you speak on the subject of your expertise and send them back to work motivated?

Being asked to be a luncheon speaker is quite a compliment! Do it well and you are a hero. Do it poorly and you're like most luncheon food . . . soon to be forgotten.

FIRST, MASTER THE OBVIOUS

For some reason the setting is never right, so your first concern is figuring out where to stand. It's not like a more formal meeting where the audience sits in one place and the rostrum or podium is set up so that the speaker is the center of attention. Sometimes ten or twenty people on the dais flank the speaker on both sides—which means you're trapped behind the lectern. At other times, the configuration of tables makes it difficult to find a central place to stand so that you are in command of the entire audience and room.

One good strategy is to let your host know in advance that you will be using slides or a PowerPoint presentation with a projector. That will force the room to have a focal point. That's where you will stand in order to use your visuals. And if you should decide you won't use visuals, don't tell anyone until the room has already been set up. Then you'll still have the spot you need.

If there are more than a hundred people, make sure you have a platform at least three feet high. You can't be at ground level with that big a crowd. They need to be able to see you for most of the talk. If you are one who likes to mingle with the masses, walking through the group as you talk, you can do so, but the opening and closing should always be delivered from a platform, where you are the center of attention.

WHAT KIND OF MICROPHONE?

There is only one answer—a lavaliere mike. Don't accept the claim that they don't have one. Don't accept the statement that they only have corded lavaliere mikes. Don't accept a handheld mike. Tell them that you MUST have a cordless.

You might argue with me on the handheld. You might be one of those people who simply must have something to hold. OK, your choice. But it's a crutch, and it limits your impact. Handhelds also have their perils: Novice speakers sometimes forget to hold directional mikes up to their mouths and, whoops, there goes the volume.

Or perhaps you are thinking, "I don't care about impact, I'm thinking about survival. I would rather speak into the stationary mike while standing behind a lectern and feel I'm being protected by something. I don't want to walk anywhere or go anyplace. It's bad enough to be giving this talk in the first place. Please don't make it any worse."

OK. You win. Survival is more important than impact. Use the lectern mike if your confidence level needs a bit more support, but promise yourself you'll work up to using a lavaliere mike next time.

SHOULD I USE VISUALS?

Visuals help get and hold attention. They help register points. We are guided by that physical rule that 85 percent of all information stored in the brain gets there through the eye. Visuals make what we say more memorable.

And, just as visuals serve as notes for the audience, they also serve as notes for the speaker. You don't have to have a written script or handheld notes if you can read them off the PowerPoint slides on the screen. You should use visuals whenever possible.

LIGHTS ON OR OFF?

As soon as we show up with a projector, the audiovisual aide will want to turn the lights way down. Your job is to tell him or her, "I want the lights as bright as possible even if they have to squint to see the visuals."

It's important to say, "bright as possible." The one thing you don't want is darkness at noon. You don't want to be a shadow of yourself up there. If there is a choice between you being seen or the visuals being seen, you win, hands down.

Remember that you are not showing Rembrandt's paintings. You are showing graphs and bullet points and, hopefully, illustrations. They should be idea visuals, not artistic works. They don't deserve center stage. You do. The most important visual you will have working to make you successful *is you*. Don't compromise with the audiovisual people or let them intimidate you. You are the speaker, a featured attraction at this luncheon—the main event. You decide how bright the lights are. And the brighter the better.

HOW LONG DO I TALK?

Brevity can be blessed. Length can be deadly. Twenty minutes is good. If they beg you to go thirty, give in gracefully. But longer than that, don't do it. Maybe at a seminar you could do it—but lunch is the wrong setting.

I recently conducted a training session for an investment banking house. We were working with sixty top producers. At noon we broke for lunch. At 12:45 the president was scheduled to speak for twenty minutes. He spoke (sitting down, no less) *for one hour*. It seemed interminable, even if it was the president. Then he asked for questions. Believe me, the sixty listeners had had enough (later on they were quite candid in telling us so), but if the president wanted questions, they were smart enough to supply them. The Q&A lasted another forty-five minutes.

That noontime break, which was supposed to be forty minutes for lunch and twenty minutes for the president, turned into two hours and forty-five minutes. But much more important, the sixty producers thought it was much too long and wasted a lot of time. So don't think that the audience is enthralled if your speech goes long. No matter who you are, or what your credentials, long is bad. The news media once criticized President Clinton when he addressed Congress for an hour and twenty minutes. Too long!

FORMATTING YOUR TALK

Obviously, you were asked to speak because you have credentials and recognized expertise. You know the subject or you wouldn't be there. The temptation for you, or any speaker so flattered, is to stuff the luncheon audience with information, drown them with facts. There's no question you should provide a lot of information, but please don't think that's everything. No speaker was ever serenaded because he or she broke a world record for providing data.

What we get serenaded for is being interesting. By and large, facts and statistics are not interesting by themselves. We use that form of evidence to increase our credibility and to support our viewpoint. We all gravitate to it because that's the way business is run. But audiences don't pay attention enough to track statistics. An audience is much more moved by a story. That is what piques their attention and sways their thinking. That is what impresses them. If you want the audience to love you, tell a story.

A much loved truism:

> *Tell me a fact and I'll learn.*
> *Tell me a truth and I'll believe.*
> *Tell me a story and it will live in my heart forever.*
> —Indian proverb

ALL THE WORLD LOVES A STORY

So find one. You won't have to look that hard. You do have to look inside yourself, and decide you are willing to share. A story is always appropriate. The entire world loves a story—as long as it's a good one and it's well told. The story needs to support your viewpoint, but it doesn't have to be a business story. As a matter of fact, it's better if it's not. But the point of the story should be consistent with the point of your talk.

Here's what to look for in reaching for a story:

An event you lived through or studied about that moved you. The more impact it had on you, the more impact it will have on your audience. If your story involves kids, yours or someone else's, you can't miss. Why? Kids are universal, part of everyone's experience. And they're cute. The story can't be a travelogue or merely a reminiscence. It must have tension, drama, and a "moment of truth" where someone's decision causes success or failure.

HOW TO TELL A STORY

There is a right way and a wrong way to tell a story. The right way is to start at a point in time. Take your cue from the most memorable stories in any culture. They all start with some variation of "once upon a time," the same way a fairy tale begins. Then let it flow.

Don't explain the story (wrong way). Re-create it the way it happened (right way). Use dialogue. Add rich detail so the audience will see what you saw, hear what you heard, and feel what you felt. Then make your point, tying it back to your overall message.

Below is an example of the same story told both ways so that you can see the difference. It is the story of a father and his daughter. To make it easier to follow, it is written in the first person, as though you, the reader, are the father telling the story.

THE STORY—THE RIGHT WAY

The occasion was a luncheon meeting of one hundred and fifty new employees of IBM. The featured speaker was an executive vice president of the company. The purpose of the talk was to welcome the new people and give them an insight into the history and the culture of the company. The executive vice president (EVP) accomplished most of that in the first half of his twenty-minute talk. Then he segued into a story to dramatize what he felt was one of the guiding principles of the company:

THE SEGUE
Now that you're a member of our company, you are one of us and we value you as we would a family member. Let me share a story with you about my own family that shows you what I mean.

SETTING THE PLACE AND TIME
It was 8 o'clock on a Friday night and my daughter, Liz, was sixteen years old. She had a date with Mark, her boyfriend. While she was waiting in the family room for her date to arrive, I asked, "What time will you be home, Liz?"

LAUNCHING INTO ACTION AND DIALOGUE
"Twelve o'clock," she replied.
    I said, "You know the rules. Eleven o'clock is your curfew."
    Reluctantly, she said, "OK, Daddy, but sometimes problems come up and I can't make it at exactly eleven."
    "Problems? What kinds of problems?" I asked.
    Liz looked up at me and said, "Like a flat tire."
    I said, "OK, if you have a flat tire, you can get home at 11:30. Otherwise it is 11 o'clock."
    Mark came to the door. I told him, "Take good care of my daughter. Make sure she is home by 11." I kissed Liz good-bye and out she went, into the night.
    At 11 o'clock, I was sitting in the family room in my pajamas and bathrobe, watching TV. No Liz. At 11:15 I thought, "Maybe she had a flat tire." By 11:45, I was angry.
    Liz came through the door at 12:15. I could hear the car tires screech as Mark backed out of the driveway as fast as he could. That was smart on his part. He escaped feeling my hands around his throat. With hands on hips, I said to Liz, "Well, where have you been?"

"Daddy, you probably won't believe this. We had a flat. We put on the spare and then had another flat tire. We had no second spare so we had to get help before we could get home. That's why I am so late."

I stared down at my beautiful sixteen-year-old daughter. I didn't buy the story of the two flats, and I think she knew I didn't buy it. She knew she was wrong. I knew she was wrong. But we both were going to have to live together in this house, as father and daughter, for a lot more years yet.

MOMENT OF TRUTH

I wasn't sure an argument would get either of us anyplace. It was after midnight, and we were both tired. It was no time to start the Father-Daughter War of the Century. I would talk to her in the morning. I put my arms around her and said, "Next time, no flats, OK?"

Liz pulled her head back, looked up at me with her beautiful green eyes, and said, "OK, Daddy, I love you." She ran off to bed.

The next morning we had a talk. I didn't accuse her of lying—nothing to be gained there. I didn't say the flats were a made-up story, or that she was being irresponsible, or that she was thoughtless. Nothing gained there either.

I did say I was worried about her as I waited there. I told her that I had complete confidence in her, that I knew she would always do what was right. I said that was why I was so worried. I knew she would call if she were detained for any reason. I knew she wouldn't be that late knowing her father was sitting up waiting for her.

Liz looked at me and said, "Daddy, I'm sorry. It won't happen again."

CONCLUSION

And, you know what, I felt good about what I had done, and I think Liz did, too. She also taught me a lesson. There's no question that giving her a fine reputation to live up to was much more effective than catching her doing something wrong and berating her for it.

. . . AND THE POINT
We try to do the same thing in our company. We consider it one of our guiding principles to trust our people and give them a fine reputation to live up to. And we have discovered over the years that almost all of us will reach higher when expectations are higher. We go out of our way to demonstrate that we are all equals as people, regardless of our titles. So if you ever wondered what differentiates our company from other companies, what makes our company great, it's that fundamental principle that will never change . . . respect for the individual.

THE STORY—THE WRONG WAY

I want to tell you a story that happened to me. It is about my daughter not coming home when she was supposed to, and I decided that you can't always resolve problems right when they happen. I always set a curfew, and my kids know that I stick by it. The curfew is 11 o'clock on weekends. My daughter had a date on a Friday night and missed the curfew by one hour and fifteen minutes. She came in knowing she'd be in big trouble and told me a cockamamie story about getting two flat tires. That was her excuse. I didn't buy it for a minute, and I think she knew it. But I let her get away with it because I thought it was too late to confront her with the obvious. And actually it worked out pretty well, because I showed her I trusted her, and she was pretty good living up to that reputation in the future. We do the same thing in our company now, and it works.

The wrong-way version is not as powerful, is it? Compare the two and you can see what it is lacking. It has no time or place established in the first sentence. This makes it hard for the audience to draw a mental picture of the situation.

There is no dialogue, so it is devoid of personality. The audience doesn't really get any impression, good or bad, of the daughter, the boyfriend, or the father who is giving the speech. There are no details that would allow you to experience the story. Even though the moral of the story is the same, we don't feel the same impact. This means that the audience is less likely to remember the point. The story is forgettable—and so is the speaker.

THE STORY SUPPORTS YOUR MESSAGE

Make sure the story supports the key message you want to leave with your audience. The only exception to this is if you are a fabulous joke teller. Then you can tell a joke story to the group even if it doesn't fit too well. But most of us aren't in that category. And it makes no sense to practice at a luncheon presentation before a large audience. As a matter of fact, unless Jerry Seinfeld has personally laid his hands on you and welcomed you into his fraternity of joke tellers, it would be prudent to drop the whole idea of going for the big laugh.

MAKE IT MEMORABLE

People generally forget jokes once they leave the luncheon room. They do remember a good story. If you were to tell that father/daughter story as a part of a luncheon talk you were giving, and let's say the whole talk lasted thirty minutes and that story lasted five, what do you think people would remember about your talk? Probably the story, right?

Members of the audience would probably come up to you afterward and say things like: "I loved the story about your daughter." "I think you handled your daughter just right." "Your daughter is lucky to have a father like you." "I wish our company respected the individual the way your company does." The reason they would say those things is that you would have gotten inside their heads and their hearts. You moved the audience, because you made your point come alive for them in the form of a story. You expanded their life experience. Audiences love that. It makes the talk special.

SHOCK THEM WITH HEADLINES

One very effective way to get the attention of an audience, especially at a luncheon, is to shock them with a headline. Make a statement that surprises, startles, or challenges them. Teenagers are great at this. My son Ryan, who is sixteen, said this in the car the other day: "I've done an experiment at school, and I've discovered that girls prefer it if I treat them badly."

Imagine my reaction. My stomach tightened, and my lips clamped shut. Does he really believe this? What kind of experiment? Where did we parents go wrong?

Ryan accomplished his objective. He had my full attention. And that's the purpose of shocking your audience with headlines.

EXAMPLES OF HEADLINES

Here are some business examples that I have seen work effectively:

"The organization is going to change in ways you can hardly imagine over the next six months."

"The compensation plan, as you know it, no longer exists and never will again."

"I have a message from our customers that negates everything we once thought was true—and you'll never guess what it is!"

There are three rules to make this technique work effectively.

1. The headline should be just that, one sentence.

2. It should hint at information that intrigues or shocks the listener and makes them want to hear more.

3. It should dramatize the topic of the discussion.

END WITH ENTHUSIASM

Don't let the audience down at the end. The end of your presentation needs to feel like the dessert they have just eaten, sweet and satisfying. Show your enthusiasm through animation and volume. Restate your viewpoint. Send them back to work with a lift.

KEY LEARNINGS FOR A LUNCHEON PRESENTATION

Do:

• Keep it brief—thirty minutes at most. Brevity is blessed; length can be a bore.

- Find a story to serve as evidence for your viewpoint. If it's good, it will be the centerpiece of your talk.
- Make the story come alive for your listeners
  - By establishing place and time.
  - By using action and dialogue.
  - By re-creating the feelings/emotions the story evoked in you.

Don't:

- Bore your audience with too many facts and statistics.
- Let the audiovisual staff run your show. Turn the lights up as bright as you can, so that *you* are displayed better.
- Hide behind the lectern. Get out front. Be dynamic.
- Use a handheld mike or lectern mike. Unless you're Phil Donahue or the president of the United States, a hands-free, cordless lavaliere is the only way to go.

5

HOW TO HANDLE
AUDIENCE PRESSURE

OMETIMES AN AUDIENCE CAN BE YOUR WORST ENEMY. It happened to the president of Exxon when he tried to explain, or perhaps apologize, for the oil spill in the Gulf of Ortiz. Certainly, some of the Enron executives experienced real hostility when facing congressional inquiries. Martha Stewart discovered audiences could quickly turn from being merely fickle to being truly hostile when insider trading accusations caused her world to turn sour. President Clinton felt the pressure during the Monica Lewinsky investigation.

It's hard to generalize on how you should prepare for big-time hostility. Each crisis has its own characteristics. Each has to be handled in the context of those characteristics. If it ever happens to you, remember that you will have time to prepare—because the rest of your world will come to a dead stop. Nothing else will matter, and you will have nothing else to do. You can either resolve the issue and reestablish your credibility, or you get your comeuppance and then fade from public view.

But let's be realistic. Most of us will never be in that kind of "us-against-the-world" situation, though we may, on occasion, have to speak to a somewhat unfriendly audience.

Let's examine this situation in a business context. Recently I was working with the chairman and CEO of a financial investment firm (let's call him Frank Jones, and we'll say the company's name is Investex) to help him prepare for his annual meeting. The meeting was to be held in St. Paul, Minnesota—not at the Investex headquarters in New York. Frank talked to me about the problem he would face and what he wanted to accomplish.

THE SITUATION FROM FRANK'S VANTAGE POINT

"The news I will be conveying is not good. The market has been volatile. We have maneuvered to try to stay in the 'black' and haven't succeeded. Our fund came in at minus 4 percent for the year. I will be standing up there in front of a highly sophisticated audience giving them that report.

"They, in turn, will be thinking, 'I pay a significant fee for Investex to manage my money in a way that creates growth. If Investex can't accomplish that, I'm paying for nothing; I've wasted my money.'" And, he added with a shake of his head, "I don't blame our investors for feeling that way."

THE SITUATION AS THE AUDIENCE SEES IT

As a first step, I asked Frank to imagine himself as a member of that audience. This was part of his apprehension—worrying about "what people would think" at the end of his talk instead of analyzing what their expectations would be as they walked into the room.

Analyzing this did not take Frank long.

"As a member of the audience I would know about the minus 4 percent before coming to the meeting," he reasoned. "As a matter of fact, that is the very reason investors would be attending. Their confidence is shaken, and they want to see if ours is too. They are not panicked yet, but they're very unhappy and annoyed."

Frank decided that most of those who would attend would be looking for reassurance that Investex was on top of the problem and in control. If the meeting didn't accomplish that, he realized, they would retaliate by moving their accounts to another firm.

FRANK'S GOALS FOR HIS TALK

Frank wanted to do something with this audience that he had never done in the past. He was always one of those straight-from-the-shoulder speakers. He gave the facts, told the business story, never said anything personal, never any humanity. He felt there was no place for that in a business talk.

But he was bothered by the fact that people seemed to shy away from him after an event. They seldom came up to him to chat or ask questions. The other speakers—the president, the portfolio manager, and the chief investment officer—didn't suffer that fate. But, for some reason, Frank had created an aura of formality. Audiences felt he held them at arm's length, that he was not approachable.

That's not a plus when you're delivering bad news.

For this speech, he wanted—in fact, badly needed—to change that. He wanted to do something that would enable him to create an emotional connection with the audience. He knew it was possible because St. Paul was his hometown, and most of the attendees would be local people.

He also wanted to put the results in their most favorable light and, in the process, break down the hostility.

GREETING ATTENDEES AND SHAKING HANDS

We talked over the situation and agreed that Frank should personally greet attendees as they entered the meeting room. The rationale was a simple one. If you shake a hand, it is far less likely that person will turn against you. The same principle applies in politics, which professes this golden rule, "Shake a person's hand and you have his vote." The rule doesn't hold absolutely, of course, but the percentages are in your favor, and it's a good way to start on a positive note.

With that in mind, Frank decided he would stand at the front entrance beginning a half hour before the scheduled start time, introduce himself, and shake hands with each person who came in. He wouldn't leave his post until he had to go to the podium to start the meeting.

MAKING AN EMOTIONAL CONNECTION

His speech that day went something like this:

> Good morning ladies and gentlemen. We are here today to talk about the performance of your portfolio, the management of your money. Money management seems so impersonal. But, as with any business, it's run by people. And I'm one of those people. So if you'll allow me, I'd like to tell you something about myself and why I'm so happy to be in St. Paul, Minnesota, with you today.
>
> To me, being here in St. Paul is returning to my roots. I was born here, not far from East Sixth Street. I graduated from St. Joseph High School, which is only a stone's throw from where we are right now.
>
> Please forgive me for the nostalgia, but I have in my hand a 1966 photo of four boys in football uniforms with "St. Joseph High School" across their chests. One of them is me. The photo was taken after we won the city championship that year. I was a linebacker, and my goal in life was to eventually play for the Vikings. I never wanted to leave this part of the country.

Frank had never spoken about himself in a talk before. But one of his goals was the emotional connection. There is no other way to do it than to talk personally. We had discussed how much he should share. He didn't want to say that he came home to bury his mother. He thought that was too personal. We agreed that anything short of that would be okay.

> But I did leave. I went to an Ivy League college for four years, coming home to see my mother and father at every opportunity. Then, at the age of twenty-two, I left for good. I went to business school and from there to New York City to make a career in the financial services industry.
>
> I wanted to come back here often. But I didn't visit much. My mother would call me every week and say, "I only see you once or twice a year. Come home. Let me baby you again. Have some home cooking. See your cousins, your aunts, your uncles, your old friends."

The audience loved the fact that he was a native son. They identified with him being torn between career and home. They loved the sharing; audiences always do. They could feel his humanity. Sure, he was the chairman of this big financial investment firm, and some of them were angry with him for this year's poor performance, but they could feel his humanity, and they liked it.

He continued:

> I consider St. Paul to be my hometown. I learned to drive on this city's streets. I played hockey on Steven's Pond. I rented a tuxedo to go to my high school prom here.
>
> Why do I tell you all this? Because what I'm doing now is revisiting my roots. Being in St. Paul again is being home for me. I know it's also home for most of you, and I wanted to share our common heritage.

ESTABLISHING THE AGENDA

Having united himself somewhat with the audience, Frank could then move on to his statement of purpose:

> But we have other matters to discuss. First, I want to speak about our performance this past year. Then I want you to hear from our president, two of our portfolio managers, and our chief investment officer. Each will present for fifteen minutes. Then we'll spend forty-five minutes or so answering your questions.
>
> Our performance—overall, we were down 4 percent on the year. It pains me to tell you that, and I'm sure you are even more pained to hear it. The market has been volatile. We have made many adjustments and corrections in an effort to stay one jump ahead. Some have worked and some have not.

It's important to state the agenda for the audience so that they know what to expect. This is especially true when the news is bad and they know it.

PUTTING RESULTS IN THEIR MOST FAVORABLE LIGHT

Once Frank had stated the obvious—that nasty minus 4 percent—the audience could be satisfied that he wasn't going to excuse or dance around the poor performance of the fund. He didn't back away from it or gloss over it. He didn't obfuscate. Asserting the problem up front and making himself responsible for it made it easier for him to move forward and share a more positive side of the same bad news:

> The minus 4 percent is an absolute measurement. If we look at relative indices, we look much better. The Standard and Poor's index was down 12 percent in that time period, versus our 4, so we outperformed the market.
>
> And when we look at the Morningstar measurements, we outperformed eight of the twelve funds in our category. When we talk to other professionals in our industry, they pat us on the back and say, "Nice going. You outpaced the market in an incredibly difficult year." What they are saying is that on a relative basis we did very well.
>
> But that's not what we are in business for. We are in business to invest our client's money wisely, to increase the value of each client's portfolio.

By adding the perspective of a favorable relative performance versus the market and versus other funds, Frank was able to end his "bad news talk" by actually putting the year's results in a more favorable light:

> As I stand before you today, I am pleased that we are outperforming most of our competitors, and I know that we invested your money wisely, but I am decidedly displeased that our fund is minus 4 percent for the year.

At that point Frank introduced the first of the three other speakers, and the meeting progressed according to the agenda. The storyline was consistent. Then came the question-and-answer (Q&A) period—another potential minefield for any bearer of bad news.

Q&A PREPARATION:
QUESTIONS, ANSWERS, AND PROCEDURES

A successful Q&A session doesn't happen automatically. It takes hard work, hard preparation beforehand. There are three steps:

1. Anticipate the questions.

2. Reach agreement on what the answers should be.

3. Rehearse the phraseology you will use to properly convey the nuances that are necessary.

ANTICIPATING QUESTIONS

Prior to the meeting, write down the questions you expect to be asked. Here is the list that Frank and his team came up with. You can see that many of these questions might fit in anybody's list, regardless of the subject:

- Is this a trend? Can we expect more of the same negative performance?

- What steps did management take to improve the situation?

- How quickly did you act?

- Why didn't you make changes more quickly?

- How does our fund's performance compare with that of competitive funds?

- How will you improve our performance in the future?

- What do you see happening in the next year?

- Why should we have confidence in you?

- What changes have you made in portfolio management?

- Is your compensation impacted by the performance of the fund?

- What was the biggest lesson learned last year?

MANAGING QUESTION FLOW

But predicting questions is not enough.

How you handle questions determines how the audience feels about everything that preceded it. They recognize it for what it is—it's the prism through which they evaluate your performance, your message, your competence, your credibility, and the success of the entire meeting.

They know it's the part of the program that is not scripted. The audience's attention is at its highest by far. On a one to ten attention scale, the talks that precede the Q&A receive an average of three or four. The Q&A session gets a nine or ten. The audience knows you are on the spot. They see you thinking on your feet. They are impressed when you do well; they are disenchanted when you flub one. But what an opportunity!

MANAGE THE FLOW BY ESTABLISHING RULES

Start things off by raising your hand when you ask for questions. This sets the norm for being recognized. You don't want people calling out questions. When the hands go up in the audience, select one person. This rule helps avoid confusion and increases your control.

You may be saying to yourself, "Wait a minute, I'd feel foolish standing there with my hand up in the air, waiting for questions." You are right when you say, "waiting for questions," because you will have to wait. The questions are not spontaneous. It takes approximately fifteen seconds for a normal audience to come up with a question.

Why the delay? Because it takes time to create a question that will sound brilliant to the assembled group. And the person who breaks the ice wants to sound brilliant. So expect the delay and be patient. The questions will come. Let's consider what to do in those fifteen seconds.

Posture. Right hand up at shoulder level, left hand forward of your body, scanning the audience. It may feel uncomfortable at first, but what's comfortable? Hands folded in front of you in the "fig leaf" position? That looks weak, tentative. Arms folded across your chest? Now you appear confrontational, aggressive. Hands behind your back, the reverse "fig leaf"? Weak again, unsure. So what to do? Use the posture recommended above. Right hand up in the "questioning" position. Left hand out, scanning the audience. It works. And, with practice, you'll feel comfortable, and you'll look strong and in control.

Content. You need to speak during the silence, during the gestation period, while someone in the audience figures out how to phrase a question impressively. But you don't have to worry too much about content. Say something like, "I'm glad we have this opportunity because I want to hear from you. You've heard from me long enough. So please feel free to ask any questions that you may have on your mind. I, in turn, will answer them to the best of my ability. I'm not concerned with controversy, so don't let that hold you back. The important thing is that we have a dialogue together."

Notice that there is nothing earth-shattering in what you have said. You are simply keeping the pressure on them, the audience. The ball is in their court, not yours. You are gently giving them time to perform, to do their part. And they will—every time. So don't panic and say, "Well then, if there are no questions, thank you and good bye." Just give them a little time.

A hand will appear. The first hand raised can be thought of as a calling card/ice breaker to stimulate others to participate. You note it and say. "I see one hand over here. I will start with that person. Anyone else?" Then another will pop up. You recognize it, "Oh, yes, we have another . . . and another over there. Let's start with the first person who raised her hand—and your question is?"

The process has begun. From there on it flows naturally. So stop worrying that there will be no questions and that you will look foolish standing there.

LISTEN FOR THE ISSUE

Concentrate on the issue, not the answer. What do you think most speakers are doing while someone is asking a question? Thinking of the answer, right? But the speaker who is trying to figure out the answer may miss the issue—which is what the question is all about. The speaker who misses the issue answers the wrong question. The dissatisfied questioner then snaps back, and says, "No, no, that's not what I asked." Ouch!

Fix your eyes directly on the person asking the question. Listen for the issue. If the question isn't clear, ask the person to clarify it: "I'm sorry, I don't understand your question."

REPEAT OR REPHRASE THE QUESTION—EVERY TIME

It doesn't matter if the answer is on the tip of your tongue, repeat or rephrase the question. Do it every time. Here's why: *This technique makes you the center of the exchange.* You are naturally the source of the answer. By rephrasing, you are also the source of the question as you heard it. This also assures that the audience has heard the question you will answer.

Most importantly, rephrasing creates thinking time for you. The human brain contains something on the order of thirteen billion brain cells (give or take a few). In the time it takes to rephrase, those brain cells are running through your mental files, looking at your storehouse of information from a variety of perspectives, and developing or selecting the answer. They (the brain cells) also are working out proper phraseology so that the answer best fits the context of the meeting.

Simple or nonthreatening questions can be treated in a simple way—repeated or parroted with an uplift of the voice, either using the same words or a slight variation.

Question: How will you improve your performance?

Repeat: How will we improve our performance?

Other questions can be rephrased:

Question: How can we have confidence that you will improve your performance in the future when this year has been so dismal?

Rephrase: Is there reason for confidence in our future together?

ANSWER THE QUESTION
Answer briefly, but don't answer yes or no. The audience wants to hear your thinking. They are not looking for one-word answers; they want a dialogue. They want to get a sense of how you got there, how your mind works. Also, don't get locked in on one questioner. The audience wants broad audience involvement and so do you. Beware being trapped in a monologue with one persistent questioner.

THE TIE BACK
The final step is to relate your answer to the viewpoint or benefits of your talk. Remember, your purpose in speaking to a group is usually to influence their thinking. That purpose would be the point of your talk. The "tie back" should reinforce that point.

WHEN THE QUESTION IS A CHALLENGE

However, there are cases when the question is really a challenge. The goal of the questioner may be to put you on the spot, or undermine you, or even topple you. You feel it. The audience feels it. The tension is high. The interest level is at its peak. The best procedure for a challenge question is to reposition the challenge by rephrasing on the issue. Let's look at the most common issues. Then we'll return to repositioning the challenge.

THE MOST COMMON ISSUES

Priority

Feasibility

Cost

Time

Competence

Why are they the most common issues? Because they are the key factors driving business strategies and decisions. Look for them during Q&A. Knowing them beforehand helps you think on your feet.

The issue of priority is close to the issue of importance and should be looked for in that context. "Why are we doing this?" The issues of feasibility, cost, and time are easier to recognize when the question is asked. Competence is often connected to quality or confidence in future results.

THE CHALLENGE IN A SMALL MEETING ENVIRONMENT

Let's examine the impact of the challenge in a small meeting environment. You are making a recommendation to a board, an executive committee, or to a group of superiors. You are suggesting something new. That's why it's a recommendation. You need approval or agreement to go forward. Often it's a way to solve a problem or to take advantage of an opportunity. It may involve a new product, a new direction, a new procedure, the purchase of new equipment, a new process, a new strategy, or creating a new department.

You present your recommendation, support it with evidence as to why it will work, and add the benefits that will accrue. Let's assume the presentation is first rate.

THE CLASSIC PUT DOWN QUESTION

Then comes the Q&A session. Most of the questions will be informational in nature. But, sure as the sun comes up in the morning, you'll be challenged with some variation of this question:

Why didn't you think of this sooner?

Suppose you repeated or restated the question: "Why didn't we think of this sooner?" Notice how that restatement traps you into a negative approach to your answer. You are almost forced to start on the defensive, such as: "The reason we didn't get to this sooner is that we were committed to another project, etc." or, "We didn't think of it sooner because our budget structure wouldn't permit it," or, "We didn't . . . because our priorities were different."

Notice how negative it all is.

MAKE THE REPHRASE NEUTRAL

You've just made a dynamite recommendation to do something great, and the momentum is sucked out of you by a negative questioner who traps you into being defensive. So what can you do? Simply rephrase on the issue. In this case, the issue is timing. The best lead in for your neutral rephrase is, "What about . . ." Then add the issue, timing. It goes like this:

What about the timing of this recommendation?

What you have done is neutralize the question when you rephrased it. You are not playing games. The question was about timing. An audience will never take offense when the rephrase is neutralized. They will not feel the question has been changed. There is no trickery to this so long as you hold true to the issue.

ANSWERING THE NEUTRALIZED QUESTION

You now begin your answer with why the timing is advantageous. Your answer begins:

Because of the . . . (Here you insert the conditions that make the timing propitious, such as economic upturn or downturn, positive cash position of the company, failures or successes by the competition, favorable publicity, etc.)

End your answer positively, with something like this:

The timing seems ideal to take the steps we have recommended.

THE TIE BACK

Go one step further; tie it back to your recommendation, and by this method turn a negative comment into an opportunity to reprise your recommendation.

Usually the transitional words "That's why . . ." lead you nicely into the tie back.

Here is a clean version of the whole exchange. Note how the answer alludes to the criticism of the original question but does not become defensive.

Question: I can't understand why it took you so long to come up with this. This is your area of responsibility. What you are suggesting could have been done a year ago. Why didn't you think of it sooner?

Rephrase: What about the timing of this recommendation?

Answer: I share your sense of the situation (indicate that you are referring to the questioner, either by name or gesture) in that I, too, wish we could have moved in this direction long ago. The opportunity seems so good. At the same time, we are blessed by the recent upturn in the financial markets, which makes the timing seem almost ideal for us to make this move now.

Tie Back: That's why we are asking for your authorization to proceed quickly to put this project into motion.

WHY IT WORKS SO WELL

There is no confrontation. The questioner has not been put down. The rest of the people at the table feel the question was answered well. You may wonder, why add the tie back? It's because you are there to sell a point of view, the recommendation. Your goal in handling the questions is to reinforce the points you made in your talk. The tie back helps you do that by keeping your viewpoint front-and-center during the Q&A.

HOSTILITY IN A LARGER AUDIENCE

Now let's move back to the larger audience situation and assume the same question came up. You, as a speaker, have learned something in this exchange. You don't want to deal with that questioner. He or she is probably a source of trouble. The challenger is probably ready to criticize and tear down the credibility that you have constructed. Therefore, when you complete your answer, don't end by looking at him or her. You certainly don't say, "Does that answer your question?"

"And why not?" you might ask. Because he or she will immediately say, "No you didn't answer my question. What I meant to ask was . . ." And you are caught in a dialogue with that one person to the exclusion of the rest of the group. On top of that, it's the one person you don't want to be caught with. Instead, finish your answer with your eyes fixed on someone on the other side of the room. Then, raise your hand to signal you've finished and to encourage other questions.

Sometimes in volatile situations, questioners will bombard the speaker with multiple questions. This happened frequently during the Iraqi war press briefings. Here's an example of a question that was raised in one of those briefings. It had many parts and much venom . . . enough to throw almost anyone.

> "We have heard that Saddam is alive but wounded, can you verify that? Also, it seems you aren't doing enough to reestablish normalcy and eliminate the looting in Baghdad. What are you planning to do about this? And how about the economic impact of the war? Businesses are dying in Iraq. Can you comment on that please?"

What does a speaker do with all that? The best way to handle multiple questions is to set up parameters at the beginning to guard against it. I would suggest saying something like this: "In order to make sure we get an opportunity to answer as many people's questions as possible in the time we have, I'm going to ask you all to please ask one question at a time."

If you still get asked a multiple question, you have the right, based on your ground rules, to make the question singular. Therefore, your procedure is to rephrase it, condensing it to a manageable morsel:

> "That question has many parts. As I hear it, the main thrust is this. What are we doing to get Iraq back on its feet so it can handle its own affairs as an independent nation with a functioning government?"

Now you can answer the rephrased question accordingly. At the end of your answer look elsewhere for the next question so that you don't get involved in a one on one with that questioner.

DON'T GET INTO A ONE ON ONE

If the offensive questioner shouts out, "Hey, you didn't answer my question," or "I have another question," simply state (without looking back) "Excuse me, we have a question over here; let's give this person a chance." The audience will side with you when someone tries to dominate—as long as they feel you are making every effort to work on their behalf.

Occasionally someone will talk for three minutes or so while formulating a question. When the talking stops you are not at all sure what has been asked. What do you do? Don't try to do the mental gymnastics necessary to fight through it and create a question so as to bring order out of chaos. Not your problem. Simply say, "I'm sorry, I didn't get your question." The burden then falls back on the questioner. Usually, the second attempt is shorter and clearer.

Do the same thing if the question is in the form of a statement. Certainly, in both those cases you have the option of formulating a question out of the debris that has been aired. But remember, it's an option, not a responsibility.

This is especially useful when handling questions in a press conference. If you find yourself facing the press, there is no need to feel awed. They are just part of the audience asking questions, and the same principles apply.

WORST-CASE SCENARIO

Let's look at a worst-case scenario. Assume you are talking to an audience of fifty people. Let's say it's the Investex meeting described earlier. There is one person present who wants to destroy your credibility and scuttle the meeting. He is sitting in the second row, right-hand side. You know he's there. You know he's bad news. He'll be the first to raise his hand. His goal is to monopolize the Q&A. Your goal then becomes to limit his participation so that he doesn't destroy the impact of the meeting.

THE HOSTILE QUESTION

Frank's presentation for Investex, not surprisingly, included a few hostile questions. Here is one:

> Question: Is it true that the management team's compensation is not performance-based? In other words, if the fund performs badly you make the same amount of money as if it performed well. There is no motivation to perform well. Is that not true?

Having anticipated the question, prepared, and rehearsed the words he would use, Frank responded like this, starting with a rephrase:

> What motivates the management team to perform well?

This was his answer:

I have put together a management team that I think is second-to-none in the financial industry. These people (and you have met some of them today) have different talents and skills. But they have one dominant characteristic in common. They all have a burning desire to excel. They want to be the best in the industry in their discipline.

Each of us is a shareholder in the same funds you are invested in. Our money is invested there because we believe that, in the long run, we are the best and our funds are the best place for our money to be. Just as we feel it's the best place for your investment dollars.

Are we bonused on the performance of our fund? Yes, we are. But that is not the great motivation. It's the desire to excel that drives us. Our lives, our careers, our reputations, depend upon it. And you, our shareholders, are served by that drive toward exceptional performance.

Frank wrapped it all up with a tie back:

> That's why we went to great lengths to show you how our performance measured up against that of other funds and the market as a whole. It is true we suffered a 4 percent decline. We regret that, and we'll strive to improve it. We know we can, once market conditions improve, because our performance, on a relative basis, was quite strong.

Notice how Frank, once again, took on the awkward question directly. No pussyfooting. He answered the question at some length, made himself the center of the interaction, and showed that he was not afraid. Is it a perfect answer? No. There is no such thing as a perfect answer. We are talking about dialogue between you and the audience, not about perfection.

How would the audience react? Probably quite favorably. How would a bad guy react? He would not be satisfied and would probably start to ask a follow-up question. But you would raise your right hand, signaling you are ready for another question. You would put your left hand out, in the stop traffic position facing the bad guy. Then you'd say, while looking elsewhere, "Sorry sir, let's give someone else a chance. I see a hand over there." Your hand acts as a stop sign. Your manner reinforces it. Bad guy will go silent. You can count on it.

You can repeat that procedure as the meeting continues. Bad guy might ask three questions, maximum. But he knows, and the rest of the audience knows, that "everyone should have a chance." Once the audience has that mindset, the influence of bad guy diminishes greatly. And you will have handled the pressure masterfully.

Because Frank and his team rehearsed beforehand, they all handled the questions well. Later on, he told me he was fascinated by the fact that no unanticipated questions were asked.

The potential hostility of the audience never materialized—once the audience grasped that Frank had the meeting—and therefore the issue—well under control. "It's amazing," he said, "how proper preparation turned a potentially difficult situation into a controlled environment and a successful meeting."

He also loved the fact that people came up to him afterward to talk about his family and ask him more about his roots in St. Paul. They loved his opening talk. They were impressed with how he and his team welcomed all the questions and handled them candidly. The result: The audience left the meeting feeling the future would be better than the past. Their money was in good hands. Their confidence in Investex was enhanced. Successful meeting.

KEY LEARNINGS FOR HANDLING AUDIENCE PRESSURE

Do:

- Anticipate questions beforehand. If you work at it, you can predict nine out of ten of what you'll be asked.
- Rehearse the answers with your experts present. Know your facts are right before you go live.
- Always restate or rephrase the question. Not sometimes. Always.
- Identify the issue at the core of the question. Rephrase on the issue.

Don't:

- Think about the answer until you have rephrased the question. If you do that, the answer will be there.
- Answer back by directly addressing the questioner. He or she will trap you with another question, and another. You want dialogue, not monologue.
- Think you can wing it without rehearsal. That's hubris. You gain nothing but could lose everything.
- Try to put down a questioner. If you're successful, the audience won't forgive you. If you're not, they won't forgive you. Either way, you lose.

6

HOW TO ORCHESTRATE THE SUCCESSFUL BUSINESS LUNCH

A FEW YEARS AGO, I was watching the 11 o'clock news. The newscaster introduced the next story:

And now, a story about the evolution of the business lunch. Can we say times two? Many busy executives are now making room in their schedules for two business lunches, back to back.

"Oh, my goodness," I thought to myself, "how could anyone pull that off? How do they get rid of the first lunch guest in time to welcome the second? Do they eat twice? Do they pretend that each lunch is their one and only?"

I sat there with more questions than the reporter covering the story could possibly have had. Were they making this all up, or was it true? I waited through the commercial break to hear the details.

It was true. A new wave had hit. Execs were doubling up the lunch window. Why? *Productivity*, they said: *Lunch meetings are a way of saying thank you to business clients, to subordinates, to coworkers, to your boss, if you want! It's also a way for two people to lower the tension bar and build a better relationship. And, lest we forget, every now and then some important business is conducted at lunch!*

The productivity crush of the 1990s embraced this time-tested tool in the excessive manner that characterized the era: "If one is good, maybe two would be better."

USING LUNCH AS A BUSINESS TOOL

Happily, there is good news for those of us who were starting to picture a world of four-hundred-pound, over-lunched executives. The double lunch didn't make it. We are back to the world we know, the once-a-day business lunch, sandwiched in between your power breakfast and that important client dinner.

How do we use this great business tool so that our time is spent well and our objectives are accomplished? It doesn't happen automatically. A successful business meal takes a bit of planning ahead of time, and the planning will pay dividends.

THE MOST IMPORTANT FACTOR: ACOUSTICS

Two of our family members are deaf in one ear. Because of that, I am unusually sensitive to acoustics in restaurants. We went to one very popular Italian place recently with the whole family—ten of us. The décor was perfect; there was lots of room around the tables so you weren't being bumped into as the waiters walked by. Restless children could actually stand up and walk around the table to entertain themselves when they got antsy. The food was served family style, with a variety of pasta and sauce—plenty of food, which could easily be shared. Garlic bread was everywhere, and the scent permeated the air. It was all good.

But the overall experience was all bad. These two family members couldn't hear. And I had trouble too! Sound seemed to be bouncing in all directions. We talked louder, trying to fight through the decibel level. We sat there and looked at each other. We nodded and smiled and pretended, in that brainless empty way that people do when they can't hear. And we ate in the silence created by all that noise.

Because love and genetics bind our family together, the experience did not harm our relationship. If you were to find yourself in that circumstance at a business lunch, you wouldn't be so lucky. The lunch, as a relationship builder, would be a failure. As a business meeting, it would be a failure. As a way to use time more productively, it would be a failure.

IF YOU CAN'T HEAR, IT DOESN'T WORK

Bad acoustics will kill a business lunch. You can't discuss an issue and reach an agreement if you can't hear the nuances clearly. And, if you and your guest are listening hard but missing pieces, neither of you will feel good about the meeting—or about the time you are spending together.

The experience becomes frustrating. The "meeting" part of the business lunch is unsuccessful. And an unsuccessful meeting always damages a relationship. Everyone ends up a loser.

Don't think you can overcome bad acoustics. You can't. Check out the acoustics first. Visit the restaurant with a friend. Have lunch at a busy time. If you have trouble carrying on a conversation, or if you have to speak loudly to be heard, cross that restaurant off your list. Don't ever give bad acoustics a second chance.

SECOND CONSIDERATION: SPACE

A while back, when I was working at Citibank, my boss, Frank, who was a group manager, took two of his direct reports (another manager, named Mary, and me) out to lunch. The purpose was to "recognize" the two of us for the great job we had done on an important project.

The restaurant had nice décor and wasn't noisy, but the tables were pretty tightly packed. As a matter of fact, I had to move my chair a little bit to the side so that it wasn't touching a chair from the next table. We constantly had to shift chairs to let the waiter get past. And Frank couldn't back up his chair without bumping into the person behind him.

The tables were also a little too small. We had a glass of wine as part of the celebration. Gradually the table was filled with the wine glasses, salad plates, main course plates, water glasses, coffee cups and saucers, butter plates, and table rolls. Fortunately, we didn't need to have any business papers on that table—there wouldn't have been room.

But back to the story. Mary and I were thrilled to be recognized in this way and to be the sole object of our boss's attention. And for half of the luncheon, that's the way it was. But, little by little, I noticed that Frank was being distracted by a conversation about football taking place behind him. The two men at the table were criticizing and making fun of the play of the New York Jets quarterback in the previous Sunday's game. It was the kind of banter you hear in a crowded restaurant. At first I thought that was typical Frank, being distracted, since he had been a college quarterback and constantly alluded to that fact in his conversations.

FRANK IS IRRITATED BY THE NEXT TABLE'S CONVERSATION
Suddenly, Frank turned around and confronted the two men at the table behind him.

"Have you ever played quarterback in college or professional football?" he asked. The startled man at the next table said somewhat defensively, "No, of course I haven't." Frank responded, "Then I would suggest that you haven't earned the right to criticize someone who has. If you don't have the talent to stand in the other person's shoes, don't criticize the way he stands in them."

That was it. He turned back toward us, and we continued the luncheon. The other people didn't say another word. No yelling. No punches were thrown. We were lucky—and relieved.

Frank explained his outburst to us: He couldn't stand to hear professionals criticized by amateurs. "They are not football players. How do they know? Let either of them be hit by a three-hundred-pound charging lineman while trying to throw a pass and see how accurate he is." Frank continued, "I'm not saying the criticisms are invalid. I just think you have to earn the right through experience to criticize someone who is much better than you will ever be."

FRANK'S OUTBURST RUINED THE LUNCH

Well now! I admired Frank's philosophy, but this was supposed to be our luncheon. Mary and I were supposed to be the center of Frank's attention. Suddenly we were sharing him with the fellows at the next table. And those fellows didn't want him. At that point I wasn't sure I wanted him either. Frank settled down after a while, said a few more nice things about us, paid the check, and the recognition lunch was over.

Naturally, Mary and I talked about the luncheon later. We were grateful to be recognized, of course, but we kept going back to Frank's outburst. That unscheduled event upstaged our luncheon. And all because there wasn't enough space. The tables were too close together.

That restaurant gets a "D-minus, never again" rating. It doesn't work for a business luncheon meeting. Tables must be spaced so that accidental contact is almost impossible, and there is no threat of being overheard. And tabletop space must be ample so that materials can be referred to during the lunch.

THIRD CONSIDERATION: THE FOOD

Thirty years ago, there was a restaurant in midtown New York called Jimmy's La Grange. It was a popular business luncheon place for the advertising agency set. The specialty was Chicken Kiev. The owner, Jimmy, would come to each table and draw the Chicken Kiev on the tablecloth with a dark pencil. Then he would give a short talk on how it was prepared and how it should be "attacked" with a knife and fork. It was popular because the food was good and there was a "special," which, despite its flashy name, was very simple.

Today, Chicken Kiev might not be simple enough for a business generation that prefers line-caught ahi tuna and bottled spring water. For a business lunch to be successful, the food must be good, but it doesn't have to be great. If we were talking about a business dinner, that would all change, and the quality and preparation of the food would be all-important. But as you have noticed, food is priority number three, behind acoustics and space at a business lunch. Simplicity is the key. If you want the gourmet dining experience, save it for after hours. Everything at a business lunch should be conducive to discussion. That's its purpose—to make conversation flow more easily, to improve the personal relationship, to discuss business issues, and, occasionally, to arrive at decisions. That's why space and acoustics are so much more important.

HOW TO PICK THE RIGHT RESTAURANT

If you are going to make luncheons an integral part of the way you do business, select two restaurants, centrally located, that meet the above criteria. You'll need two if you plan to have business lunches three days a week or more. Have lunch at each with a cohort from work. Introduce yourself to the maitre d', or the owner, or the headwaiter, as the case may be. Let's say his name is Armando.

Tell Armando you'll be lunching there frequently and that you would like "that table" (pick the one that would seem to work best for you). Ask him how you should identify that table when you make a phone reservation. He will probably answer your question by saying, "Ask for table number twelve" (or some other identification). Thank him by name, hand him your business card, give him a generous tip, shake hands, and say you'll be seeing him next week.

ARMANDO WILL GREET YOU

Next week when you arrive with your guest, Armando will greet you by name. (You may think that's going too far, but it's not. Don't knock it until you've tried it.) You will sit at the table you selected. You will receive impeccable service. You will be much more relaxed because you now know the place; you have the "home field advantage." Your guest will be relaxed because the restaurant is perfect for the purpose. You will accomplish more than if you were scampering around town taking potluck at different restaurants.

When you leave, thank Armando and give him another tip: the same amount every time. Don't begrudge him the money; this is how a maitre d' makes a living. From your vantage point, think of it as though you were renting a very special office space. This real estate, with its amenities, is worth many times as much as the gratuity—you're really getting it for a song.

TIMING—START IN THE OFFICE

If you intend to conduct some real business over the noon hour, schedule your luncheon meeting to begin at 11:30 A.M. at your office. Schedule the restaurant for 12:30 P.M., and don't worry too much about getting to the restaurant on time. Armando will know you are coming. Your table will be there.

But you have done two things. You have the perfect environment for holding a productive meeting—your own conference room. All the materials, all the people you need, are there. You have also created an interesting psychological advantage. You and your client will both be working toward a 12:30 P.M. deadline. A subtle pressure has been created. Chances are you will accomplish more in that hour than in a normal three-hour meeting.

TIMING—FINISH AT LUNCH
Don't expect to finish all of your business before leaving the conference room for the restaurant. It doesn't happen that way. You will both decide you can't do everything in that hour, and certain subjects will have to be addressed over lunch. Nothing to worry about. That's the way it should be. The beauty of the follow-up lunch is that it obviates the delay that normally comes from needing to schedule another meeting on another day, yet it still provides a bit of a break between sessions.

The restaurant meeting becomes more productive than ever because it has a running start. The food will be good. Armando will make sure the setting and the service are exceptional. You will both be feeling good about what has been accomplished so far. The acoustics are good, so you can hear one another. You have plenty of space. It's a setting that is most conducive to making decisions or reaching important agreements.

WHO PAYS?

The answer, as they say, depends on the circumstances. Let's examine some of them:

Supplier takes client to lunch
This is simple. The supplier is expected to handle the check unless there is an overriding reason (anniversary, birthday, etc.) to do otherwise, or unless the client states that his company's code of ethics does not allow it.

Senior executive takes juniors out to lunch
As the title implies, it's the senior's show, unless prior agreement states otherwise. The juniors expect to be treated. "After all," they think, "the senior exec is making a bundle and can probably expense it anyway." If you don't want it that way, you have to discuss it first. Otherwise it's automatic.

Business acquaintances have lunch

A simple predialogue takes care of this. Agreement should be reached on the restaurant (pricey or not), on who else will be there, and on who pays. Asking the restaurant to split the bill between two credit cards is now a widely accepted practice. If it's a male and female, it's essential that the issue of who pays is agreed on beforehand.

Forget the old thought that the man automatically pays. Chivalry doesn't apply when the woman and the man are equals. Work it out first, and then enjoy the meal and the company.

If the situation is a sticky one and you want the treat to be on you, consider borrowing a process from many private clubs. They don't deliver a bill to the table. That way the whole process is invisible. The member pays.

You can make a similar agreement with "your" restaurant. If this is helpful (and many women in business have told me it is), all you have to do is make arrangements with Armando to charge the meal to your credit card, which you gave him when you entered. He'll return the card to you as you go out the door. All will be handled professionally and gracefully.

Your guest may still put up a mock fight and feign displeasure, but this will vanish as soon as you go out the restaurant door and the fresh air hits the both of you.

TO DRINK OR NOT TO DRINK?

If the boss takes you out to lunch and he or she asks what would you like to drink, the answer is, "iced tea."

There is an exception. If you are being celebrated and the boss has a glass of wine or beer, you can do the same. Drink it slowly and refuse seconds, even if the boss has another—or a few more.

That may seem overly stringent but consider this: The lunch is an opportunity to score points. There is nothing wrong with a glass of wine, but why press it? In Europe it would be different. But in this country stay with the iced tea at lunch. Do your heavy drinking later.

ANOTHER CONSIDERATION—BREAKFAST MEETINGS

Bankers invented these. Think about it. They're not as functional as the business luncheon described above, but they are sometimes easier to arrange, and they have a lot of value.

Breakfast tends to be shorter, with fewer interruptions for various courses and such. There is less on the table, so you can more easily carve a workspace. The duration is shorter, so you will both feel you are using your time wisely. And no major crises have yet arisen to cloud your focus and ruin the day. No wonder they're called power breakfasts.

THE ICEBREAKER

We always wonder what the "icebreaker" conversation should be about when we are out with a client or with senior people in our own company.

The *New York Times*, with the help of BBDO advertising agency, had a great advertising campaign years ago that encouraged folks to read the *New York Times* to aid them in their business discussions. The headline was: "Did you pay your share during lunch yesterday?"

The campaign was a play on words. The point was that a good lunch partner (or breakfast partner) contributes to the content of the discussions. So make sure you "pay your share" and are well-read on the day's events, especially in the areas of interest to your lunch guest.

Tom Hill, a management supervisor at Communispond, says, "A well-read individual will add value to any encounter, if you have the ability to express yourself clearly and persuasively. You will always be sought after as a breakfast, lunch, or dinner companion."

You will be considered interesting. People will seek you out. Now, isn't that a nice way to stand apart from the crowd?

KEY LEARNINGS FOR ORCHESTRATING THE SUCCESSFUL BUSINESS LUNCH

Do:

- Start the meeting in your office, one hour earlier, so you make progress and go to lunch with momentum. Both meetings will sparkle that way.

- Plan what you want to accomplish at the premeeting and the luncheon. Improvisation is for the theater and doesn't work there that often. Don't rely on it for a business meeting.

- Preselect your restaurant—so good acoustics, ample space, fine service, and a solicitous maitre d' are all standing by.

Don't:

- Think charm alone can make a lunch meeting successful. Charm lasts for five minutes. The lunch will take an hour-and-a-half. Plan it out and have an agenda.

- Expect to get it all done at lunch. Instead, start with a one-hour office meeting. Then the lunch part will be really productive.

- Use a business lunch to try out a new restaurant. Egad, that's so foolhardy it deserves to be punished. And it will be.

7

HOW TO SELL YOUR IDEAS

F OR MANY YEARS I WORKED WITH JAMES KINNEAR, the president and chief executive officer of Texaco, during the most challenging period of its history. James Kinnear was an Annapolis graduate, a decorated Korean War hero, and one of the most effective executives I've ever worked with. He was speaking on the subject of ideas one day and said:

A good idea isn't worth a darn, unless you can sell it to someone else.

As I heard that statement, I thought to myself, "Those words should be put on a plaque and hung in every office." We have to be able to sell our ideas or they die. So is there a better procedure for selling an idea? Darn right there is. In our Communispond Executive Presentation Skills Program we suggest a format.

HOW TO SELL AN IDEA FORMAT

1. Problem Cause
2. Negative Effects
3. Idea Recommendation
4. Benefits to the Audience
5. Evidence
6. Summary of Recommendation and Benefits (3 and 4)
7. Calendar Action

But let's not just take that on faith. This format has been taught to thousands of executives who have used it effectively, and I have, too.

THE PRESENTATION STORY: INCREASING VICKS SALES

At the Vick Chemical Company (now owned by Procter & Gamble) I was the product manager for Vicks Vaporub in Canada. My job was to increase sales of venerable Vicks Vaporub—a mentholated salve sold as a cold remedy—through advertising. I was supposed to start by identifying obstacles to growth. In other words, identify the problems. Well, one of the problems was that sales of this forty-year-old product were declining and had been for some time. I knew what had to be done, or thought I did—just get those sales up.

DON'T SETTLE FOR THE OBVIOUS
When trying to identify a problem we often grab onto the obvious. If we were to go into a thousand business conference rooms on this day, the day you are reading these words, we would hear some variation of the same statement: "The problem is that our sales are down." In most

instances that is not a clear enough statement of the problem to point us toward a solution.

We need to dig down beneath the obvious, to find the cause or causes of lack of growth. It might be because of a big turnover in the salesforce, or that our new people are untrained. It may be because of misdirected advertising, or that our competition has a great "price-off" offering. The trade may be responding to incentives that promote a competitive product, or an out-of-stock condition may exist. There may be delivery problems. There are many, many possibilities.

IDENTIFY THE PROBLEM, BEFORE THE SOLUTION

When I sat down to begin to formulate a solution, I thought about Charles Kettering, one of the great men in industry. His inventive genius is credited by many for having sparked the growth of General Motors early in the twentieth century. Kettering trained himself to never begin by looking for a solution. He would always focus on identifying the problem in terms of its primary cause. He would start by gathering information that would continue to define, and therefore narrow, the problem.

Kettering felt that the apparent problem (declining sales) was often not the real problem. He advised that we dig deeper and find the causes and then frame the problem statement in those terms. He believed that then the problem statement would point us toward the solution. One of his statements is quoted in business schools across the nation.

A problem well-stated is a problem half-solved.

So in my responsibility as product manager, I began by following Kettering's advice of gathering information to narrow the problem.

GATHER INFORMATION

I studied our company's research. A nationwide survey of cold product usage over a two-year period had just been conducted. There were some remarkable bits of information in that study, including this:

- Vaporub was in 93 percent of homes (almost no other product is in that many homes!)

- The average use-up rate of a jar was fourteen months (very few other products take so long to be used). Five years earlier it had been ten months.

- The favorable/unfavorable rating for the product was 97 percent favorable. (Mothers loved Vaporub; they just didn't use enough of it).

There was a lot more information than that (some sixty pages more), but the startling revelations were contained in those three useful facts.

There were two other important facts. One was that all of our advertising was geared toward persuading the mother to buy the product. (But she didn't have to buy it. In 93 percent of the cases, she already had it in her medicine chest!)

The other fact was that sales of Vaporub were slowly declining and had been for the past five years.

DON'T RUSH TO CONCLUSIONS

I looked at all that information and thought to myself, "Wow. Our sales have been sliding for five years. Our advertising is way off-base. It's stupid. It shouldn't be focused on getting consumers to buy the product. Our dollars are being wasted. The agency should be fired. The copy message should be to use more when they use it. Or to use it for additional purposes."

I flustered on. "Our goal should be to increase the use-up rate of the product; maybe we should suggest that the customer throw it out after a year; or maybe we should decrease the size of the jar so it doesn't last as long, or change the formula so that it spreads more, or disappears into the skin so that they use more. Maybe we should advertise that the product be used for sore muscles . . ."

Whew! You can see the flights of fancy I became involved in—the tendency to rush to a solution—to come up with an idea. Charles Kettering would have disowned me.

USING THE ORGANIZATIONAL FORMAT

Let's fill in the organizational format, outlined earlier in this chapter, using the Vicks Vaporub example so that you can get a better feel for how the pieces fit together. Here is how the ideas were narrowed down, researched further, honed and polished, and finally presented at a meeting to Vicks senior management:

1. Problem Cause

The goal here is to look beneath the obvious problem. In our example, Vaporub's sales were dropping. That would seem to be the obvious problem, wouldn't it? But it's too broad. It's not directional. It shoots us off in all directions. We need to dig deeper and find the cause of that obvious problem. What is causing the decline of sales? That's what Charles Kettering meant when he said, "A problem well stated is a problem half-solved."

The initial research provided a real target to work on. The problem cause in this case is a slowing in the use-up rate of the product: it now took fourteen months, instead of ten months, to use up a jar. So the problem cause statement is:

> The jar, which is in 93 percent of the homes, takes fourteen months to use up.

Is that a perfect problem statement? Probably not. But it's pretty good. The focus is entirely on use-up rate. Notice that no person or department is attacked. The problem is almost detached from its contributors or its perpetrators. I could sell that statement of the problem inside the corporation because no one would be defensive about it.

THE PROBLEM STATEMENT REVEALS AN INSIGHT

The statement of the problem almost always represents an insight, beyond what is superficially obvious to the onlooker and thereby creates real interest. Obviously you should have additional information that supports the problem. In this case we could share the following:

> Half the users (mothers) dip two fingers into the salve and spread the product lightly on the child's upper chest only. They don't spread it on the back or the nose. They are less satisfied with the product than those who use more.
>
> Also, they stated that they had never thought of the possibility of applying Vaporub beyond the upper chest. It had never been suggested.

These facts were followed by the good news:

> Forty percent of the users spread Vaporub on the back as well as the chest. They are more satisfied with the product and the results than the first group.

On average they use twice as much as the first group.
The most satisfied users are those who are most lavish in
the amount of Vaporub they spread on the sick child. This
group, on average, uses up a jar in seven versus fourteen
months.

Those facts are important. Notice how they amplify the problem. They
don't compete with it or muddy it.

Why should we spend so much time on identifying the problem?
Because this is the most important step in developing the idea solution. When the problem is presented with great clarity, the listeners
understand it better than they ever did before. The listeners can accept
the fact that the problem is a worthy one. Ultimately, the solution will
fit, hand in glove, into this new understanding.

In effect we will have "sold" two important parts of our idea format to the assembled listeners. The first is a new perspective on the
problem. The second is the germ of the idea that will solve it.

2. Negative Effects

Negative effects are the signs that something is wrong.

In our example:

The overriding negative effect is that sales have been
declining for the past five years.

Notice the negative effect is what we first misidentified as the problem. You can often list a number of negative effects, but be sure they
all are caused by the same problem. Negative effects are often painful.
They tend to cause a wringing of hands, a gnashing of teeth. They are
the bad news, as well as the setup for the next step in the format.

3. The Idea Recommendation

The idea is your recommended solution to the problem. You should be
able to state your idea by completing the sentence, "The idea is . . . "
Naturally, you will want to go further and describe the various features
of the idea. But make sure your statement of the idea is crystal clear
and as simple as you can make it.

In our example:

The idea is to change our advertising emphasis one-hundred-and-eighty degrees—from purchase to usage.

Notice how simple the statement is. It's easy to understand. It's dramatic. Yet it flows directly out of the problem and the negative effects.

GIVE AN EXAMPLE TO FLESH OUT YOUR IDEA
It's always important to give an example of an idea. It increases understanding. Don't worry about letting the cat out of the bag. This is no place for coyness. So in our case:

An example of the kind of advertising copy that would flow from the new strategy is this: "Apply Vaporub to the back as well as the chest for two times more soothing warmth, two times more vapor medication."

INCLUDE NEGATIVE FALLOUT FROM THE IDEA
We should also be clear about the ramifications of the change we are suggesting. We don't want to mislead by omission. By all means, outline some of the negative fallout involved in enacting the idea. By being up front at this early point we demonstrate that we have examined the total picture and are making the recommendation with eyes fully open. We come across much stronger for doing so.

In our example:

But we need to recognize that the enactment of this change in copy is not without some difficulty. It would mean that all existing advertising would have to be mothballed and new advertising created for television commercials, print ads, billboards, and point-of-sale materials. The unbudgeted out-of-pocket cost would be significant. At the same time, the benefits would seem to far outweigh the costs.

4. Benefits to the Audience
When selling anything—especially an idea—it's always good practice to clearly state what the benefits will be to your audience. It doesn't matter if your audience is one person or a roomful of senior managers: Tell them how their life could be better if they sign on to your plan.

In the Vaporub presentation, it went something like this:

The benefits of this change in advertising would be:

- A conversion of 20 percent of the "front only" users to "front and back" would translate to a 10 percent increase in volume used. Sales would increase commensurately.
- Our advertising would concentrate even more on the mother-child relationship, since Vaporub application by the mother would be the main idea and the new focus of the ad campaign.

The result would be:

- The user satisfaction with the product would increase.
- The efficacy of the product on the sick child would be greater, since more of the salve would be applied, and more vapors would be inhaled.

The benefits of your idea solution should reverse the negative effects and perhaps provide added or unexpected value. Here, the unexpected value is a real heart-warmer: Little children with sniffly noses will feel better because Mother used more of the product!

5. Evidence

Here is where we demonstrate that our idea will work. As we discussed in Chapter 2, there are five forms of evidence: Personal Experience, Analogy, Judgment of Experts, Examples, and Statistics and Facts. You can remember them all with the simple mnemonic, PAJES.

SELECTING FROM THE FIVE FORMS OF EVIDENCE

Personal Experience—First-person testimony. An incident out of your life that supports the point you are making. In a business presentation, this narrative can be a report of the research you did on the problem or an anecdote relayed from the folks in field sales.

Analogy—A point of similarity between two unlike things. For example, the tip of the iceberg analogy conveys a warning about seeing only a small portion of something and missing the significance of the whole. The racehorse analogy used in Chapter 2 illustrates how effective even a brief analogy can be.

Judgment of Experts—A statement by a recognized authority that appears to be supportive. For example there are two experts quoted earlier in this chapter who would fall into that category (James Kinnear and Charles Kettering—see how easy that is?)

Example—A specific situation with various key factors similar to those of your premise. Examples are persuasive to the extent audiences see them as paralleling your own case. In this chapter, we'll show how an example is used.

Statistics/Facts—Numerical or other facts arranged for analysis and interpretation. Graphs help your audience appreciate relationships between numbers. Choose pie charts if you want the audience to see percentages, bar charts for comparisons, line charts for trends.

USING EVIDENCE TO SUPPORT THE IDEA

Now back to the Vaporub story. The evidence of the example was used to support the idea of increased usage, suggesting to mothers that they use the product on both the front and the back of the child.

Let me show you why we're confident that the idea will work.

During September, October, and November we conducted a pilot test in Sudbury, Ontario. We selected one hundred homes. We picked up their Vaporub jars, and replaced them with full ones. The customers were happy because they ended up with more Vaporub than they had before. We didn't tell them about the test. We did the same thing in one hundred homes in a control market.

THE VAPORUB "FRONT AND BACK" ADVERTISING TEST

For three months we ran special "Vaporub, front and back" advertising in Sudbury. Our regular old advertising ran in the control market. Then we picked up all the jars again and replaced them with full ones.

We melted down the contents of the hundred jars from Sudbury and compared it to what we obtained from the melted down jars in the control market.

The Sudbury test market had used 14 percent more Vaporub.

We examined and reexamined the test. It was clean in
every way. That's why we are confident that our recommendation is solid and on target: Vaporub "Front and Back"
advertising will increase sales.

It's important that your evidence supports the idea recommendation by showing that your solution is likely to bring about the benefits.
Do not use evidence that merely proves the reality of the problem. At
this point the audience accepts the problem as real; they don't need to
see graphs and charts that show declining sales. They should see the
graph or chart that shows how the Sudbury experiment raised product
usage by 14 percent.

6. Summary (of Recommendation and Benefits)
The summary should be brief. In our example, the first sentence sum-
marizes the idea recommendation:

In summary, we recommend that the company change
Vaporub's advertising strategy from what it is currently,
which is product purchase, to product usage.

The second sentence reprises the benefits to the audience:

By doing so, we anticipate a sales increase of 10 to 15
percent.

The key point here is to restate the idea in one sentence. Restate the
key benefit only.

7. Calendar Action
Finish your idea presentation by stating one action that will get the
ball rolling. When should it happen? Put it on the calendar:

The recommended next step would be to schedule a
meeting with the advertising agency, share this presentation
with them, and begin the change process. With your approval,
I'd like to schedule that meeting for Tuesday of next week.

As you can see, the format enables you to present your thinking in a
persuasive and logical manner. The presentation should be short in time
(ten minutes is usually enough) but long on persuasive content. The

Calendar Action step assures that your work will not be in vain; your listeners will have to make a decision—and you have an advantage.

KEY LEARNINGS FOR PUTTING TOGETHER AND DELIVERING A TALK TO SELL IDEAS

Do:

- Look for the cause of the problem. That's really what you solve—the cause, not the problem.
- State your idea recommendation in one sentence. Until you can do that, the idea is not clear.
- Use a format like the one suggested so that your presentation flows persuasively.
- Keep the presentation short. Fifteen minutes is the outer limit. After that, your brilliance is not registering.
- Be enthusiastic. Show you believe. Show you care. If you don't care, they won't care. I guarantee it.

Don't:

- Assume that the audience understands the severity of the problem. Don't skip over the negative effects. Your listeners need to feel pain or they are less likely to embrace change.
- Assume your idea will sell itself. Instead, select one or more forms of evidence to support your case.
- Ramble. The impact of the tight presentation will leak away.

8

HOW TO SPEAK
ON THE SPOT

PICTURE THE SCENE: You are a senior manager of Acme
Bank. Your name is Barbara, and you have been asked to
attend a meeting on the subject of a new customer satisfaction survey. You are one of fourteen people around a
conference table. The senior vice president of human
resources, Marie, is running the meeting. She opens the meeting with
a statement of purpose:

"The purpose of this meeting is to show you the research
results from the latest customer satisfaction survey, get your

perspective on the severity of the problem we face, and generate thoughts on what kind of action our bank should take."

A LAPTOP PRESENTATION
She follows with a laptop presentation showing the following:

	Acme	Competition
Overall satisfaction	76%	87%
Satisfaction with employees	72%	84%
Total customers (this year vs. last)	−3%	+6%
Percentage of existing customers selecting a new service	22%	63%
Teller satisfaction	76%	88%
ATM satisfaction	90%	92%

Marie solicits input from a few of the attendees. Then she turns to you and asks, "What do you make of this, Barbara?"

YOU ARE SURPRISED
Your first response is a somewhat startled look. That's a pretty normal reaction. This situation is always a shock to some extent, but it is a fairly frequent scenario for all of us as we rise in stature within our companies. Maybe it's a staff meeting, maybe a marketing meeting, an operations meeting, or a weekly status report meeting.

The title of the meeting may differ, but one thing is constant: The environment is high visibility. Your boss is there; so are department heads, senior VPs, and even the president, occasionally. From a career perspective, this is center stage. Your day-to-day performance on the job is below the radar screen to many of these people. Your performance in this meeting and meetings like it is what they see. It will shape their sense of you. It will color their judgment.

THE IMPRESSION YOU MAKE
If a future raise or promotion for you has to be approved by one of these attendees, their perspective will be influenced by the impression

they get of you in this meeting. Jack Welch, the former CEO of General Electric, said it all in his statement:

"Whenever I see a young man making a good presentation, I never forget that young man." Then he paused for a moment and added, "Unfortunately, the opposite is also true."

So, for you, the meeting is an opportunity. If you handle yourself well and contribute in a positive way, the impact will stretch far beyond the moment in that room.

It is possible that you, dear reader, would handle this situation flawlessly. But for purposes of this chapter we will explore first the wrong way, then the right way, to respond. Let's repeat Marie's query, "What do you make of this, Barbara?"

WRONG WAY: PLAYING IT COOL

You, Barbara, are sitting comfortably around the conference table, a little slouched, your hands in your lap. Naturally, you are startled by Marie's query. But you like to convey the impression that you are comfortable and not awed by the stature of some of the senior people attending the meeting.

You look down and begin to respond with your eyes on your notes. You want to appear cool and unfazed, perhaps even detached. No way do you want to appear emotional. Your volume is low, no emphasis.

Your response sounds something like this:

"Something must be done when we see numbers like that. If we keep losing on these competitive indicators we'll slowly slide below the top three. Nobody keeps coming back to a bank that begins to get a bad reputation. We need to do something fast."

Not bad. But, not good either. And it has to be good to make an impact. There was no structure to what was said. Furthermore, Barbara showed no positive physical presence, which would demonstrate confidence and add value to the statement. We can't argue with the content, but it doesn't go anywhere. It doesn't do anything for Barbara as far as her career is concerned. The impression she made was mostly a neutral one.

Now here is a challenge for you. Look away from the page and see if you can remember what was just said by Barbara. Yes, you remember she expressed a feeling that was consistent with the research report. She bemoaned the current state of affairs. She said, "We need to do something." But she said nothing of substance, nothing specific—nothing impressive or memorable.

That's what tends to happen if we speak on the spot without having thought it through ahead of time, without using some simple principles to increase our impact. Yet these are the moments when the spotlight is on us. These are the moments when we are most visible within the company.

THE RIGHT WAY

There are four physical presence principles governing participation at a meeting.

First—Sit forward on the chair, back straight.
Why do we say this? Because your job is to be interested and committed to both the subject-at-hand and the audience in the room. And you should look the part. You may think you should appear unfazed and comfortable. But comfort is not the point here.

You can look comfortable for the entire rest of the day—after the meeting is over. On a scale of one to ten, with ten being the highest, looking comfortable registers a value of one in this setting. Looking interested registers a ten. Being involved registers a ten. Your job is to look, and to be, interested and involved.

Assume the president was asked for his or her impression of you after the meeting was over. Here are two comments the president could make. You pick the one that feels better: "Barbara looked comfortable in her chair, didn't she?" Or, "Barbara was eager to contribute, wasn't she?"

Second—Keep your hands above the table.
The only gestures the listeners can see are the ones when your hands are in sight. Gestures are important. They are as natural to the speaking process as words are. Whenever we speak one to one on a casual basis, we gesture without being aware of it.

Gestures will happen no matter where your hands are. They help make the speaker more interesting, more real. They show that you care. So be easy on yourself and good to your audience; let the hands do what they want to do, but don't hide them from view.

Another point: When our hands are folded in our laps, we tend to slouch our shoulders and hunch our backs. Weak impression.

Third—Focus your eyes on one person.
Focus your eyes on one person at a time when you speak. When you come to a natural break in your comment, pause and take a breath while moving to another person. That way you look much more confident and you will be able to read your audience as you share your thinking with them. If you have to consult your notes, do so in silence, then look up. Focus once more on a pair of eyes and begin speaking again.

Many people get in the habit of constantly looking down at their notes. They don't really read them. But it becomes a way to avoid eye contact. Not good. You look unsure, less credible. There is an old saying about how to handle yourself when speaking at a meeting, "Don't talk to your notes or the tabletop. Neither will respond."

Fourth—Speak up!
Forget being conversational. Conversations take place in bars or diners or at the luncheon table. You are speaking to a group. Your volume must be strong. On a scale of one to ten, ten being bell-ringing loud, you should be at a six. Strong voice, strong gestures, strong message, strong performance.

We sometimes think that a soft voice will convey intelligence or confidence. We think back to a time when we saw a senior person, perhaps the president or the chairman, remain silent for most of a meeting. Then the senior person gave his or her opinion in a soft voice, and everyone leaned forward to hear. We were impressed. The natural conclusion to draw is that a soft voice makes an impact. And it does, as long as you are the most important person in the room. The reason is that title and power create highly motivated listeners. The audience strains to hear, because of the importance of the speaker. But, if you don't have the big title, forget it. A soft voice works against you.

Think of yourself as giving a stand-up talk, sitting down. As a matter of fact, if you can stand, without violating the setting, you should opt to do so. In either case you need to speak with energy if you are to capture and hold your listeners' attention.

ORGANIZE AHEAD OF TIME

You may be thinking, "How can I get organized when this is such an impromptu environment?" It may be impromptu, but the subject is seldom a surprise. At least it shouldn't be. You should know the subject of any meeting you are asked to attend. If you don't, you should take steps to find out. How do you find out? Simply by asking the person who called the meeting. Why are you asking? So that you can be better prepared to contribute.

Will you always be smiled upon for asking? Yes, unless it's an announcement meeting where the information is intended to be a surprise, with no interaction expected.

But you'll know when that kind of meeting is in the offing. The scuttlebutt and rumors will probably run up and down the halls, days in advance, making the ultimate announcement somewhat anticlimactic.

WITH KNOWLEDGE COMES RESPONSIBILITY

We have a responsibility to ourselves (probably to our company as well) to consider the information, decide where we come out on the subject, why we feel that way, and what should be done about it. And that simple little format is what "Speak on the spot" is all about. So let's explore the format and see how well it works.

ON-THE-SPOT FORMAT

1. Issue (subject)
2. Point of view
3. Evidence
4. Suggested action

---

1. Issue. Identify the issue that is at the core of the subject being discussed. There are probably fifteen possible issues contained in the customer satisfaction report. Marie hasn't told you which one to speak to. You can't speak to the general subject of the survey and have an impact. Your message should focus on one core issue, and it can't do that unless you take ownership of the subject by rephrasing it so that it is focused for you. By doing so, you focus the audience's attention on the issue you will speak to. You also position the audience for your viewpoint, which will follow.

You might think that you should start with your point of view because that's what Marie is asking you for. Don't do it. Own the subject first by reframing it in terms of the core issue. That way everyone knows what you are talking about. You will feel much more in control, and your listeners will be much better able to follow your line of thinking.

Let's go back to our example. When Marie asks you,

"What do you make of this, Barbara?"

You begin,

"I see the issue as being customer dissatisfaction with our employees' service whenever they interact with them."

2. Point of View. Your point of view should be concise. It should be simple, easy to understand, and hard to misunderstand. Use simple words. If you can say it in one sentence, that's great. Two sentences are OK. Three is too many.

Use a lead-in such as "My point of view on the subject is . . ." Or, "The way I see it is . . ." The lead-in is a natural segue to the viewpoint. It helps carry the audience to the next step in your thought process.

To continue with our example, Barbara says,

"My point of view is that we should work to improve our satisfaction rating at every point where our employees interact with the customer. We cannot compete in the marketplace with that critical measure lagging."

3. Evidence. Now Barbara needs to support her viewpoint. That's what evidence is all about. It supports or substantiates a viewpoint or a claim or an idea or a recommendation. It adds weight. It increases the credibility of the presenter and significantly increases the impact of the presentation. If we leave evidence out of the mix, our viewpoint is only an opinion. And opinions are a dime a dozen.

As discussed in Chapter 2, there are five forms of evidence you can select from: Personal Experience, Analogy, Judgment of Experts, Example, Statistics/Facts. In a more formal presentation we might use three, four, or even all five of these forms of evidence to support your viewpoint.

But when we speak at a meeting, that would be too much. The audience would be put off by it. *We should talk for thirty to sixty seconds.* No more. We are not trying to conclude. We are trying to contribute. One piece of evidence is enough.

Barbara uses another segue to lead into her evidence, "The reason I feel this way is . . ." The role of the segue is to make the transition between thoughts natural and conversational.

Barbara speaks:

> "The reason I feel this way is that I worked for a small bank in Lima, Ohio, fifteen years ago. We had conducted customer satisfaction surveys regularly over the years. On the subject of satisfaction with our employees, the trend was a declining one. In my last year the number had slipped to 68 percent. A new bank, First National, opened up in town. Within three months we lost 30 percent of our customers. It seemed that they were unhappy and only habit was keeping them with us. When the new bank came in that was the catalyst. Boom! They were gone. Incidentally, First National still exists in Lima. The bank I worked for doesn't."

Barbara has used the personal experience form of evidence. It's a good choice. Most of our viewpoints are based upon our experiences. So why not reach into that personal inventory and use them as evidence?

But Barbara isn't finished with the evidence step. She needs to tie it back to the viewpoint so that it will have maximum impact on the listeners. She adds the "tie back."

THE TIE BACK

> "What this experience tells me is that once a customer satisfaction rating gets really low—and 72 percent is really low—we are in grave danger and must take immediate steps to improve that rating."

Notice that the "tie back" answers the question, "What is the significance of your evidence?" or "How does that apply?" It is a reaffirmation of the viewpoint in light of the evidence. It reinforces the viewpoint and helps the evidence hit home.

4. Suggested action. You can't leave your audience up in the air. You were asked initially, "What do you make of this, Barbara?" In response, you've narrowed the subject to the core issue, stated your viewpoint, shared a personal experience as evidence, and tied that back to your viewpoint. All that's left is for you to suggest a course of action.

The lead-in should be simple and natural, such as, "Here's what I think we should do . . ." or "The action I think we should take is . . ."

Let's follow Barbara through this step:

> "What I think we should do is, first, share these research results with every service person in the bank and let them know how serious we think this is. Second, I think we should establish some sort of goal like 'We must get the rating from 72 percent to 85 percent within three months.' And, third, we should create a new customer service training program and make attendance mandatory for everyone who has contact with the customer. I know this may sound heavy-handed to some of you, but we must reverse this customer satisfaction trend."

HOW DO THE SENIOR PEOPLE REACT TO BARBARA?

Now put yourself in the shoes of the president or senior VP attending this meeting. They see in Barbara a person who obviously cares about the welfare of the bank. She is a contributor, and management loves contributors. She is not afraid to speak out. Her thinking is organized. She looks impressive. She speaks in an impressive way. She handles herself well in a challenging environment. She has ideas and is willing to put them out there. A pretty solid and positive reaction.

And how do you, Barbara, feel about what you have done? Well, you stepped forward and spoke your mind on a critical issue the company faces. You didn't do it off-the-cuff, though the other attendees will be impressed with the fact that it appears you did. You were able to present a thoughtful perspective because you did some homework before the meeting. You also used a simple format, which enabled you to structure your response to Marie's question in an impressive way. The end result is that you took advantage of an opportunity to contribute to the company and to gain recognition for yourself.

That's how careers are advanced in this world we live in. Nice going, Barbara.

KEY LEARNINGS FOR SPEAKING ON THE SPOT

Do:

- Find out beforehand what the meeting is about. Think through your viewpoint. Be prepared for the impromptu situation. That's what distinguishes us in life.
- Use the speak-on-the-spot format to organize those thoughts. It will make your comments—and you—more impressive.
- Be a physical presence. Sit up straight, speak up, focus on one person at a time when speaking. Save the slouching for later.
- Seize the opportunity the meeting provides. Be a mover and shaker. You are smart enough; you know how to do it. Why let others steal the glory?

Don't:

- Start with your viewpoint. Instead, start by rephrasing the subject. It gives you ownership of everything that follows.
- Think you can wing it. Spend the time. Prepare. Do it right.
- Drone on. Sixty seconds is plenty of time. Your goal is to contribute, not to bore.

9

HOW TO MOVE
A GROUP TO ACTION

WHEN I WAS THE MANAGEMENT SUPERVISOR on the Whitehall Laboratories account for the J. Walter Thompson advertising agency, I was a participant in the most successful presentation designed to move a group to action that I have ever seen. Let me describe the situation so that you can feel the reality of it. We will stop at various points to draw lessons from what was accomplished.

Whitehall Laboratories was a division of American Home Products. One of the products we created advertising for was an antacid named Bisodol. It was a second-tier brand, but it had potential, we thought.

One day just before noon, I was working at my desk at the advertising agency when I got a phone call from the senior vice president responsible for marketing and advertising at Whitehall, Hank Peterson.

Hank said, "Kevin, I know there is no good way to say this, but we are unhappy with the creative product your agency is putting out. Bisodol sales are not growing. We feel it's because of poor advertising copy, so we are putting the Bisodol advertising account out for solicitation by other agencies."

WE WERE FIRED

I said, "Hank, what you're telling me is crushing news. I need to hear more. I'll be over there in fifteen minutes. Will you see me?" He said that would be OK. So I hustled over to their Third Avenue office to find out what was going on.

Simple enough. No animosity. We were out. Fired. Some other agency was going to get the business. Four other agencies had been invited to make a presentation. But being pushed aside on this small product meant there was danger we might lose the whole account, which was worth about $10,000,000—a pretty big account in those days.

I decided I'd better call an account team meeting to discuss the situation, so I charged down to Alan Gilburne's office. Alan was the copywriter on the account, and a darn good one at that. We called in the head creative guru, Dave Boffey, and the head media man, John Sisk. I told them the story.

Step 1: Identify assignments. Pick your team. If you're planning to move a group to action, you're not doing it alone. It's a big job. The final step is standing in front of the assembled group and motivating them, but a lot of setup work precedes it.

We spent the rest of the day analyzing the brand's marketing plan, its sales, the media plan, and the creative approach. Our immediate goal was to identify the problem and reach agreement that we could correct it. We all concluded that the creative approach was the problem. If we could solve that, we had a beginning. Our ultimate mission would be to make a presentation that would change our client's mind. We wanted the account back.

Finally I said, "We have two jobs. My job is to get Whitehall (the client) to invite us to participate in the solicitation process. Your job is to develop a showstopping creative approach that will win the shoot out and let us keep the account.

"Assuming we get the opportunity to present, we will be trying to persuade the entire group of client people who are in that room to rehire us. They won't want to do it because we have already failed in their eyes.

"We have to move them to action as a unified group. So if there are ten of them, then all ten have to vote for us. That's the only way we'll get it. It has to be unanimous. If we do well but not great, we'll lose. If there is a lot of discussion, we'll lose. We are a long shot, no doubt about that. But, hey, I'm pretty sure I can do my part. Can you do yours?"

"No question about it," they said, "we're eager to get started."

CALENDARING THE MEETING

The next day I sat down with Hank Peterson and said, "Hank, I understand that we have been fired. We are no longer your agency for Bisodol. I am not here to argue that point.

"But an amazing thing has happened. The head of our creative department has taken this personally. He has given an assignment to five copy teams to come up with a—and I'm using his words—'breakthrough campaign idea for the brand.' He's establishing a contest. The winning team goes to dinner at Lutece." (This was true, but it was mostly window dressing. I was working with Alan Gilburne, who was my number-one copywriter, and I was confident that he would solve the problem.)

I continued, "Here's my question. If we come up with something that's truly a breakthrough, do you want to see it?"

"Of course I do," he said.

"Hank," said I, "if I can come back here and look you in the eye and say we have an idea like that, will you allow us to compete for the business and present to your committee?" He agreed and went so far as to say that he would schedule us for next Thursday, a week hence, 10:00 A.M.

"I'm doing that," he said, "because I know full well you are going to tell me you have a great idea no matter what you come up with."

Since I was on a roll, I asked for the eleventh-floor training room instead of a conference room, because it was a bigger room and I hoped to generate a large audience. Hank had said we would be the last agency presenting. But his final words were killers.

"Understand," he said, "this is a courtesy only. You have no realistic chance. You are really wasting your time."

Meaning we could make a presentation but it would be to a mostly empty room. All the people who mattered had already written us off. In all probability, none of the bigwigs would come. I would have to correct that, and it wasn't going to be easy. But, first, we needed content. We needed a great message, a story line.

Step 2: Make sure the message is finely honed and finely crafted so that its promise exceeds the audience's expectation. The group must be lifted to move in the direction you want. Only the most eloquent message will accomplish that.

Or, as they say in the advertising business, we needed a dynamite creative product. It took a while. Great ideas always do. But we only had a week to come up with the idea, put the television commercial in storyboard form, and put the whole presentation together. After studying the product, the competition, talking to medical consultants, and a top-notch chemist, Alan came up with a copy claim we thought was a winner:

> Bisodol turns burning stomach acid into a harmless water solution.

It was strong, it promised a benefit, and it contained both the problem and the solution. It was short, simple, and understandable. We did a quick research test to see if it played well with acid indigestion sufferers. It did. We were happy.

There is a lesson here. If your goal is to move a group to action, make sure your message is worthy of the moment you have created. If it's competent, but not great, you are a loser. It must be startling, unique in its perspective, exciting. Otherwise the audience won't be excited.

VISUALIZING THE MESSAGE

Next we needed a way to visualize, to dramatize, the statement. We were talking television advertising here. The visual demonstration was all-important.

Alan said, "Well, if the product does what it's supposed to do, we could get two beakers. Put stomach acid (hydrochloric acid) into both, then put Bisodol into one of them and stir it around so that the chemical reaction takes place and neutralizes the acid. Then we could put a daisy into each beaker, with the petals sitting above the glass."

One of the daisies would wilt and die; the other would be fine—we hoped.

We got the beakers. We got the stomach acid. We got a dozen daisies. In Alan Gilburne's office we went through the whole thing. And, by golly, it worked.

We had a winner. One piece of the puzzle was in place. I met with Hank and told him we had a breakthrough. He said he looked forward to seeing us on Thursday.

Step 3: Decide what people you need to be present and take steps to get them there.

A great presentation to the wrong audience is like a tree falling in the forest with no one to see it or hear it—it has no significance. We had to be sure we had the right audience. We carefully handpicked the people we wanted in attendance:

Chairman of the board—William Laporte

President of the division—John Culligan

Senior vice president, marketing manager—Hank Peterson

Corporate vice president, creative consultant—Florence O'Brien

Corporate marketing guru—Ken Byrne

President of the in-house ad agency—Dan Rogers

How to get them there? "It's impossible," said Henry Schachte, the president of J. Walter Thompson. "The only meeting you could get all six of those people to attend would be their company's annual meeting."

"Good point," said I, "but we have to try. If only half of them come, we'll still be ahead of the game." My reasoning was that if I could get half of that austere group to attend, the lesser lights (though still very important people) would knock down the doors to be there.

Two people on the list were a must—John Culligan, the division president, and Hank Peterson, the senior vice president of marketing—because they were directly involved in the decision-making process. But, ideally, I wanted all six because they represented power and, if they leaned our way, the others would as well.

HOW DO WE GET THEM THERE?

Our team met to discuss what our options were to get them there. Here is the list we wrote on a chart:

- Ask Hank (the client) to invite them
- Phone each and invite
- Send a notice of the meeting inviting the recipients to attend
- Write a personal letter of invitation to each person and then follow up with a phone call

The last strategy won the day. Since I knew each of the people on the list, it was decided that I should write the letters of invitation. Here is what I wrote:

THE LETTER

Dear (Name),

I am writing to invite you to attend our agency presentation for the Bisodol account on Thursday morning, March 16th, at 10 A.M., in the eleventh-floor training room.

I am writing you personally for two reasons.

First, I know you admire great advertising and recognize it is one of the factors that has helped make your company so successful. The advertising we will show is bold. It's revolutionary. It's dramatic. In my opinion, it's great advertising. But you be the judge.

Second, four other agencies will make presentations, hoping to be awarded your business. I know the decision-making process is not an easy one. You would prefer it if one agency really stood out from the others.

With that in mind, I will make you a promise—on Thursday, the 16th, you will see a creative presentation that stands out above the four—that stands with the best you have ever seen. I'm not boasting, though it may sound like it. But I am profoundly impressed with the work we have done for you. It will make your decision an easier one.

Henry Schachte, our president, backs me up on that promise. He will also be in attendance at the meeting and looks forward to seeing you, if you can attend.

Since we are expecting a full room, I want to have name cards at the main table for you and a few other senior people. To that end, I will call your office on Tuesday to see if you are able to attend.

Sincerely,

Kevin Daley

RESULTS OF THE LETTER

I followed up on Tuesday. All six said they would attend.

Eureka!

We spread the word throughout Whitehall, the client company. Before long, our meeting became the hottest show in town. On Thursday we had the six I personally invited, plus six others, a total of twelve Whitehall people—the highest number of client attendees for any of the presentations. The most any other agency got was eight.

Additionally, there were four of us from J. Walter Thompson. Dave Boffey, the creative guru; Alan Gilburne, the copywriter; Henry Schachte, our president; and me.

But before we get to the meeting, let's look at some of the little things that would help make it go smoothly.

Step 4: If possible, unite the audience with some kind of unifying symbol so that anyone who sees the symbol knows that person was there.

We were lucky in that we had a visual symbol that was integral to the presentation. The daisy was going to be the star of the show in many ways. All of the audience's attention would be focused on the daisy during the demonstration. One daisy would die, one would live, demonstrating the efficacy of Bisodol.

Alan suggested we pin a daisy on the lapels of the attendees when they came in the room. They wouldn't understand the significance until later, but that was all right. "It would sort of bring them together," he said. That was a big idea in its own right. We decided to do just that.

Alan was given the responsibility for buying the daisies and being sure they were on site on Thursday. He also was responsible for knowing how to snip the stems and insert pins so that we would have sixteen lapel flowers, plus a dozen full-stem ones, enough for the demo plus spares.

Step 5: Get there early. Rehearse on site.

We made arrangements for the Whitehall meeting room to be open for us at 8:00 A.M.—two hours before the scheduled start time. We arrived right on time with all our paraphernalia. It was important that we get everything done ahead of time, including an on-site rehearsal. Nothing was more important in our lives right now than this meeting. No sense cutting corners and letting mistakes slip in. Here's what we did:

- Set the chairs and tables up so that they formed a partial semi-circle focused on the demonstration table in front
- Set up the demonstration table with our beakers and stirrers, our stomach acid vial, our Bisodol bottle, our vase of daisies, a pair of scissors, a pair of rubber gloves, paper towels, and rags
- Set up our storyboards on an easel
- Set up another easel to display our marketing strategy, copy strategy, rationale for the demonstration, and why it would be a competitive advantage
- Set the nametags on a separate table

Then we rehearsed the entire presentation. We left nothing out. Alan and I both flubbed some of our dialogue the first time and had to go over it again. The demo worked flawlessly. I practiced pinning daisies on the lapels of my three cohorts so that my fingers would know how to do it when the Whitehall people came in.

We felt confident. You may wonder why we rehearsed again. We had already gone through this a number of times in our office.

This entire process of doing a run-through on site is called "taking the news value out" of what we will do. We don't want news during a performance; we want routine.

One of the things that causes nervousness is a physical unfamiliarity with the setting in which you are forced to operate. Little things come up that you don't expect, such as dry Magic Markers or not enough paper on the flip chart. There is no substitute for physically doing everything in rehearsal that you will be doing for real later.

PROVIDING NAMETAGS AND NAME TENTS

We greeted each Whitehall person with a friendly handshake, a thank you for being there, an introduction to our team, a nametag with the name printed large and bold (I didn't want our president calling someone by the wrong name), and a daisy. I escorted each person to their individual chair, each marked with name tents.

You may wonder why both tags and tents. Name tents are easier to see when standing in front of the room, handling comments or questions. It's important to use the name of the client in any exchange. But at the end of the meeting, nametags let your team members say thank you with a name attached to it as they shake hands good-bye.

PINNING THE DAISY

I did the "pin the daisy" honors personally for all twelve client attendees. I didn't want them to decide whether they would put it on or not. I wanted it on their lapels, front and center. I made a special point to show my appreciation to each of the six who had responded to my personal invitation.

Each attendee was intrigued by the daisy. "What's this for?" they asked. "It's a key part of the presentation," I said. "You'll see what it stands for as we go along. But, hey, it looks good on you, doesn't it?" Which it did. So, as the meeting began, all twelve Whitehall people and four JWT people were wearing daisies.

Step 6: Make sure your top person has a role to play in the presentation. Otherwise, his value is diminished, he's just a spectator.

Henry Schachte, our president, opened the meeting. Henry thanked the attendees for the opportunity to present to them. He said that Whitehall was an important client to JWT. Bisodol was an important brand. He said, "We put the Bisodol project out to five creative teams at the agency. We set up a contest. The advertising we will present to you was the unanimous winner. We are proud of this work, and we are proud of the creative team that did it." With that, he introduced the creative team of Dave Boffey and Alan Gilburne.

DISCUSSING THE COPY CLAIM

Dave and Alan discussed the copy claim and the creative strategy behind it. Then they presented a storyboard (schematic) representing the future television commercial. The concept of the wilting daisy was explained and discussed. The audience liked the claim. They liked the thinking, and they liked the daisy idea, but they were not at all convinced that the demo would work.

During the discussion of the storyboard, all twelve observers, from time to time, looked back at the assemblage of "stuff" on the table in the front of the room—the two empty beakers, a glass stirrer, a vase with a dozen daisies in water, a pair of scissors, an opaque pitcher with stomach acid written on both sides, a roll of paper towels, and a pair of rubber gloves.

All that stuff had been there since the meeting began. The attendees were somewhat mesmerized by it. The anticipation was palpable. At some point they knew we were going to do something with all that stuff.

THE DEMONSTRATION

My role was to do the demo, which I had rehearsed six times back at the advertising agency and once more this morning. I told the group that I would re-create the demonstration for them in the same way it would be seen in the television commercial we envisioned.

I identified each item on the table, emphasizing that the pitcher contained pure hydrochloric acid, which is exactly the chemical known as stomach acid. This is what causes the burning feeling of acid indigestion when the stomach is acidic. What Bisodol does is cause a chemical reaction that turns burning stomach acid into a harmless water solution, thereby ending the discomfort of acid indigestion.

TELL THEM WHAT THEY ARE GOING TO SEE
I lifted the pitcher and filled both beakers. I removed four daisies and cut the stems so that each would be seven inches in length. (The attention level was remarkable. They stared as though I were doing an appendectomy.) I explained to the audience that the length was important because we wanted the flower to be two inches above the beaker while it was alive and then sag dramatically as it died.

I put a cut daisy in each beaker. The audience was silent to the extreme. Nothing in the room moved at all . . . except the daisies, which wilted, sagged, shriveled, and died. The audience gasped.

TELL THEM WHAT THEY SAW
I waited almost a minute before taking the next step, because the audience was so absolutely taken by the death of the daisies, which certainly dramatized how unfriendly stomach acid could be. Then I removed the two dead daisies and said, "This is what we would expect,

since the same acid that burns your stomach burned the life out of these two flowers."

I shook two Bisodol tablets out of their bottle onto the table and then put them in one of the beakers. I used the stirrer to crunch the tablets as I stirred the solution, explaining that both Bisosol tablets had to dissolve completely in order to turn "burning stomach acid into a harmless water solution." I put a Bisodol nametag on that beaker so that there would be no confusion. Then I took the two remaining cut flowers, one in each hand, and held them above the beakers.

BUILDING ANTICIPATION

I waggled the one in my right hand above the Bisodol beaker, saying, "This daisy should be fine because the stomach acid is now harmless." I waggled the other flower and said, "This one, however, doesn't have the Bisodol advantage." All eyes watched. Silence in the room. No movement.

I dropped the two daisies into the beakers. The Bisodol daisy stood tall and healthy. The other one wilted and died. I thought the demo was over, but the audience kept staring at the Bisodol daisy, the one standing tall in the beaker. The audience didn't move, no clearing of throats, no shifting in the seats, no sound. Nothing but silence.

One of the product managers was the first to speak. "How long will it stay healthy like that?" he asked. I was a little bit startled. I didn't expect the question, and I didn't know the answer. "Until long after this meeting is over," I answered. They chatted and joked among themselves. The mood was ebullient.

THE CLIENT SPEAKS

Bill Laporte, chairman of the corporation, stood up, shook Henry Schachte's hand, and said, "I've been in this business for thirty years, Henry, and I don't think I've ever seen a more dramatic presentation. I wish we could put it on television just the way we saw it today."

Then he shook my hand and said, "Kevin, thank you for pulling all this together. We saw some things today that we didn't think were possible."

I shook his hand and thanked him. I was even more grateful for the way he spoke his mind in front of all the others. What a lift that was. Now all the others would feel free to say good things.

But the meeting wasn't over. I asked Bill if he would sit down for just a minute, explaining that I had something important to say in conclusion.

In a meeting of this kind, it's important to ask for a specific action, a specific timeframe. Be clear. Don't assume they know what you want, even if it's obvious that they do. You still have to ask.

Step 7: End the meeting by telling them what you want. Be clear. You've earned the right.

I ended by saying, "We are confident that this advertising approach for Bisodol is unique and will impact the brand in a positive way. It's dramatic. It's attention-getting. It will lift Bisodol to the front line of antacid products. It will grow the brand.

"I want to add a personal note. We stand in front of you with great respect for Whitehall and great enthusiasm for what's to come. We want to be reappointed your agency for Bisodol. We want to continue to serve you. We feel we have shown you that we have the creative muscle to do the job. We want your business.

"I have one final question," I said. "When will you let us know?" Hank Peterson handled that one.

"Monday noon," he answered. They filed out with much glad-handing and conviviality. Each of them shook hands with Henry Schachte and thanked him for being there. I removed the nametags and shook hands with each of them myself. Each was complimentary. Some were effusive in their praise. I felt like I was running for office. Once the room was empty of clients, we babbled about how well it went. It was Henry Schachte, our president, who cut to the chase. "If they are still wearing the daisies at four o'clock this afternoon, we're in," he said. "And Kevin," he continued, "you better get over there this afternoon and see as many of those people as you can. We don't want to give them a chance to change their minds."

At three o'clock I went back over to Whitehall. I stopped in to see Hank Peterson. He was very complimentary, though he didn't commit himself, but he was wearing the daisy. I visited each of the special six whom I had invited. They were all eager to talk about how much they liked the idea and how they thought it would impact the brand. Most important, the daisies were still on their lapels. Now we just had to wait until Monday.

WHITEHALL'S DECISION

On Monday, Whitehall announced its decision. We were reappointed the official agency on Bisodol. The unofficial tally was twelve votes for us, no votes for any of the other four agencies. What a heady feeling that was. We had persuaded a whole group to act as one. We had done what seemed impossible.

The example above applies to an advertising situation. But the principles are universal and apply in any business environment.

KEY LEARNINGS FOR DELIVERING A PRESENTATION TO MOVE A GROUP TO ACTION

Do:

* Make your message a showstopper. If it's not that way at first, hone it until it is.

* Decide who you want the audience to be. Then invite the most important attendees with a personal letter.

* Make sure they know your top person will be there. It makes the meeting seem more important and will increase the attendance on the other side. It's crucial if you are to attract their top people.

* Create a demonstration to sell your idea, if you possibly can. It rivets an audience. Nothing else can achieve such profound attention.

* Unite the audience, if possible, with some kind of visual symbol (like the daisy) so that your message is alive all day long or until they remove the symbol.

* Rehearse any demonstration until you can do it without a hitch. Then do it one more time. Nothing is more impressive than confidence when doing a demo.

* End the meeting by asking for the action you want the attendees to take. Don't leave it to inference. Ask them specifically.

Don't:

* Run an interactive meeting without nametags or name tents. You'll never recover from calling someone by the wrong name.

- Conduct a demonstration until you've rehearsed, rehearsed, and rehearsed. A botched demo means you're an amateur—and people don't like to do business with amateurs.
- Think you can show up for this kind of meeting at its scheduled start time. Instead, get there an hour early, take the news value out of the room, and rehearse in the actual environment.

10

HOW TO BRIEF
THE BOSS

I F YOU ARE MOVING UP THE CORPORATE LADDER, there will come
a time when you will receive an assignment from someone
much higher in the chain of command. The "big boss" might be
the president of the company, or a senior vice president, or your
boss's boss.

The important difference is that it's not your direct boss who is
giving the assignment. It's not someone you are used to. An assignment from a senior person beyond your norm can be very significant
for many reasons, not to mention for your career. What do you do?

How do you handle yourself? Who else do you involve? Are there any rules for this type of thing? What are they?

That's what we'll explore in this chapter. To help set the framework, we'll begin with a story and draw some pointers from it.

THE BRIEFING

As product director for Richardson Vicks Company, I was responsible for the Clearasil brands. The president of the division was John McLaughlin, an extremely smart, buttoned-up executive.

I didn't report to John; my boss, Dick Secrist, did. Nonetheless, John had given me a special assignment to evaluate the feasibility of introducing a "makeup base" product under the Clearasil name for teenage acne sufferers. I was to report back to him in three weeks on a Thursday. And when John said Thursday, he meant Thursday.

When the due date arrived, I wasn't as ready as I should have been. I found out that John was going on a trip and was leaving for the airport at noon. So I thought to myself, "Maybe I can finesse old John McLaughlin a little bit. I'll give him a fast status report, and he'll have to leave before he can pin me down to too much detail." So I phoned Beverly, his secretary, and made an appointment for 11:45 A.M. She said she would call me when John was ready (I was just down the hall).

At 11:44 A.M. the phone rang, and Beverly said John was ready, which meant that I should be there within the minute if I knew what was good for me. My first words to John, who was a nitpicker for exactness, detail, and professionalism, were, "I know you don't have much time so I'll make this as fast as I can."

THE BOSS SPEAKS

Before I could go a word further he said, "Let me put this meeting into some kind of order. First, it is not I who does not have much time. It is you. You only have thirteen minutes, at the end of which I will leave regardless of where you are in your discourse.

"Second, I am not interested in how fast you can make the meeting go. I am looking for a top-line digest of the research you have done. I want you to articulate what your conclusions are on the matter, and I would like you to suggest the direction you think we should take. Now, if you are prepared to do that in the time you have remaining, proceed.

If not, please schedule a meeting at another time when you can provide me the information I need."

The meeting was over. John caught his plane. I went back to my office to lick my wounds. I sat there for more than an hour, stewing and feeling sorry for myself. What a jerk I had been. John McLaughlin had given me an opportunity to advance my stature with him and within the company. I had dropped the ball. I had advanced nothing. If anything, I had lost a point or two.

How many chances like that am I likely to get? I was depressed. And why was I thinking I had to go it alone? I had a direct boss. His name was Dick Secrist. He was a good guy and very supportive of me.

"Why hadn't I kept him in the loop?" I thought to myself. "He works with the president all the time. He's been around. His thinking would be helpful. So would his presence in the meeting. Besides, he's my supervisor. He's supposed to know what I'm doing. If I ignore him (which I had done beautifully, thus far), it will tick him off, and I'll lose my most valuable ally."

I spent the rest of the day working on my presentation so that it would fit the guidelines John had laid out. It was obvious I needed more information, so I made a series of phone calls to gather what was necessary.

MEETING WITH MY DIRECT BOSS

The next day I went over to Dick Secrist's office and told him the whole story of the John McLaughlin meeting. He was not impressed.

"Why weren't you better prepared for the meeting?" he asked.

I tried to justify my behavior by explaining how busy I was.

Dick said, "I don't want to preach to you, my friend, but whatever you had as priority number one becomes priority number three as soon as the president gives you an assignment. The reason it slides to number three is that the president's project becomes priorities number one and two. Nothing else you do is nearly so important."

A COMPANY HAS ONLY ONE PRESIDENT

He continued, "You can explain your way around a missed deadline with anyone else in the company. But not the president."

I didn't fight. I knew he was right. I told him I was embarrassed and annoyed with myself. I apologized and said I had learned my lesson.

Then he said, "I have one more question . . . why didn't you go over this with me before your meeting with John?

"Suppose John had asked me what I thought about the makeup base idea. What was I supposed to say? If I said I didn't know anything about it, I'd look foolish, wouldn't I? John would expect that you had been keeping me informed. And interestingly, you'd look foolish too, wouldn't you?

"You could have hurt us both. So tell me, did you intend to keep me in the dark?" I blundered through an apology. I had no intention of hurting Dick Secrist, or myself for that matter. I had been thoughtless and, when you get down to it, irresponsible as well. I didn't try to excuse myself. I told him I was wrong.

Dick said, "Chin up, boy. I forgive you." He told me he had made a similar mistake in his last company. He said he wasn't properly prepared for a meeting with his president, and he tried to wing it. The president wasn't impressed.

"It took me a long time to recover," he said. "Every meeting in that office is important. It's not just twenty minutes. It's the most important twenty minutes you'll spend that month."

Next, I told him what my thinking was on the project. He helped me a lot by changing my direction in places, challenging some of my conclusions, and suggesting changes in some of the charts I was thinking of using. I felt increased confidence, realizing that he was totally on my side. I also understood that if he was not on my side, I would have lost the battle . . . no matter how good my thinking was.

I asked Dick to join me at the next meeting. I realized his presence would add importance to the meeting, and his support would make me stronger in the eyes of the big boss. Heaven knows, I needed all the support I could get after the last debacle. Dick said he would be glad to come.

I was buoyed by the fact that, going forward, I had a better relationship with my immediate boss, who would be a supporter instead of a critic.

I went back to my office, gathered all my information, and put it into presentation form. Big news first, details second, recommendation third. I squeezed it down so that I could do the whole thing in ten minutes.

THE NEXT MEETING

Then I phoned Beverly and got a twenty-minute slot on John's calendar the next week. I asked her to mention to John that Dick would be with me in the meeting. I had learned that John was one of those, "I don't like surprises," people, and I didn't want Dick's presence to be a surprise.

The day arrived. Dick and I entered John's office right on the minute. We went through a little social chitchat, perhaps less than normal, since John always seemed to feel that was not a good use of time.

I started the business meeting by saying, "John, when we met last week you said you were looking for three things: a top-line digest of the research I had done, my conclusions based on the research, and a suggested direction or next steps on the project. I am prepared to do just that, and, depending on the level of discussion, I see the meeting taking no more than twenty minutes."

John smiled, said, "Go right ahead, Kevin."

I started. It's nice to start a presentation with the big boss smiling. It's also nice to follow a format that is so obviously a good one. The meeting proceeded without a bump. We finished in twenty minutes, believe it or not. I had more work to do, of course, but the project was going forward.

A HAPPY PRESIDENT

At the end of the meeting John said, "That was a first-class meeting. Your thinking is solid. We might really be on to something here."

My president was pleased. My immediate boss, Dick, had made some important observations that John had agreed with, so he was a happy man. And I was on cloud nine.

Dick and I went back to his office and rehashed the whole thing the way you do after you have had a successful meeting with the president. At the end of the recap he said we had learned three things. He took out a yellow pad and wrote three headings with space under each one. We talked about each, and he wrote some more on the pad.

When we were finished he gave me a copy of what he had written and kept the original for himself. He called it "Lessons Learned." Here's what it looked like:

- Prepare. Do the work. Structure it. Know it cold. Presenting to the big boss is playing in the big leagues. Never underestimate the opportunity.

- Show him you're prepared. Tell him what you are going to cover and how long it will take. It shows discipline. It shows intelligence. It's impressive.

- Demonstrate that you have listened to him, that your work has been guided by what he said. The more of him you get into your presentation, the more impressed he will be with you.

Years later at Communispond, we did a lot of research on the "Brief the Boss" subject and formalized the presentation procedure.

But before we get into that, let's examine the situation from both perspectives.

THE BIGGER PICTURE

First, consider what is at stake for the boss in assigning you this project:

You are bringing the boss information and probably suggesting action steps. If the boss decides to make a decision based on your input, the business, for which he is responsible, will change to some degree as a result of the meeting.

So the big boss needs to be reassured that you're deeply into the subject; that you've done your homework; and that you are reliable, responsible, and trustworthy. Your boss's personal reputation is at stake. It always is. New data always involves risk.

So does working with new people. And, unless the boss has worked with you a lot in the past, the boss may not know how to read you.

This is what is at stake for you:

You are in the spotlight. The boss will be examining you closely, making judgments about you. If you do well, your career will be impacted positively. If you drop the ball, you probably will not be able to recover with that company. It's not fair, but it's real. You can't change the way the system works.

So you'd better give it your best shot. Nothing else is more important to your career than how well you handle this kind of special assignment. And your "Brief the Boss" meetings will be the setting in which the boss evaluates you, your thinking, and the state of the project you are on.

Consider this the background as you approach the meeting. Here are the steps we teach in our Communispond Executive Presentation Skills programs:

Step 1: Reestablish the priority of your project.
The best way to do this is to actually quote the boss. Quote a statement he made to you about the importance of the assignment and its timing.

Remember what we said above, "The more of the boss you get into your presentation, the more impressed the boss will be with you."

Recognize that the boss has other things vying for top level attention. A lot has happened in the company since you got your spot on the calendar a week or three weeks ago. Your assignment may not be as urgent now as it was then.

But it's your project and you think it should be. Quoting the boss on the subject reestablishes the project's importance:

When we met last week you said . . .

Step 2: Lay out the agenda. Make it short. Make it time-bound.
The agenda is headlines only. Once again, you're thinking of your boss's time. You are pleasing your superior immediately by showing that you are prepared and in control. Define up front the items you are going to cover. Any boss who wants to add or subtract topics will do so right there.

And if the meeting is short, "God bless you, my child" is what the boss will be thinking.

BRIEFING FORMAT (MEETING TIME—TWENTY MINUTES)

1. Top-line digest of the research
2. What conclusions we can draw
3. Suggested next steps on the project

Put the agenda on a chart—no more than four items. It should stay visible for the entire meeting. The boss sees where you are and where you are going. You can recap using the agenda chart. He or she can refer back to an earlier item using the chart. Everyone is a winner.

Step 3: Flesh out the headlines with vital details.
The vital details are those the boss needs to know in order to make sound decisions. But be selective. Give only "need-to-know" details. If a boss wants more, a boss will ask.

What makes details vital? Details are vital when changes are indicated. Details are also vital when the boss wants to be able to predict outcomes, or wants you to.

No data dumps, please. Be selective. You're not holding back because of ignorance. You are holding back because of knowledge, the knowledge of what's important. Less is usually better than more . . . unless asked. Then be prepared to discuss the subject in as much detail as the boss deems necessary.

Step 4: Stick your neck out. Suggest action.
Many times you are only being asked for an update, a status report. Sometimes you are being asked for a recommendation. In both situations you should recommend the course of action you think is indicated.

And why is that? It's because the whole business process is about change and adjusting to change—about problems and finding solutions to problems—about opportunities and moving quickly to take advantage of them.

All of these circumstances require action. Remember the great statement of Aristotle:

Knowledge is not power until it is turned into action.

The way to make a real difference in the boss's life is to recommend actions to improve the situation that you just gave your report on. That way you have turned knowledge into power, assuming the boss agrees. If he or she doesn't, don't be surprised if the boss goes on to explain his or her own solution or his or her preferred next steps. Either way you will be the catalyst for action on the part of the boss. As such, the boss will appreciate your contributions and perceive the meeting was a good one.

And, hey! That's not all bad.

KEY LEARNINGS FOR BRIEFING THE BOSS

Do:

- Invite your direct boss to participate in the meeting, or at least meet with him or her beforehand to gain perspective and advice.
- Reestablish the priority of the information you're about to report by quoting the boss on the subject, actually using the boss's own words. There's no better way to get his or her attention.
- Establish your agenda. No more than three points. Include estimated time. No more than twenty minutes. At this point the boss will relax. You won't be there long enough to bore him.
- Cover the big picture only. If the boss wants more, you'll be asked.
- Suggest action or next steps, even if that is not part of your assignment. If you omit this, you are a messenger. Messengers are not important cogs in a company and they are not paid well.
- Finish five minutes early—in fifteen minutes instead of twenty. The boss will love you. You'll become part of the company's folklore.

Don't:

- Wing it or take it lightly. It's the big boss you're talking to. It's your chance to impress.
- Bypass your direct boss. Careers are made in these meetings— you need all the help you can get.
- Overstay your welcome. You can bask in the sun later; don't bask in the boss's office.
- Try to show how much you know by drowning the boss with information. Your boss will be bored, not impressed. And if you're boring, you won't get invited back.

11

HOW TO DELIVER BAD NEWS

"I 'LL NEVER FORGET THAT DAY!" my friend Joan said to me. "I have never felt so sick to my stomach about any message I had to give the staff as I did that one."

I'm sure many of you can guess what she told me next. Joan works in the financial services industry. Her company was "right-sizing." People would lose their jobs, offices would be consolidated, budgets would be cut, as the organization decided where to focus its spending. Life, as her staff had known it for many years, would no longer exist.

A manager's job is to communicate to staff. That means delivering the bad news along with the good. Unfortunately, for most of us, delivering the good news is a job we like—delivering the bad is a job we'd like to delegate!

KILL THE MESSENGER!

Delivering bad news is complicated. The implications are often not clear. The message is sometimes incomplete. The impact, in the larger sense, may not be known yet. And we may not be the originators of the news, only the messenger. And you know what people say about the messenger . . .

We have a lot to lose.

THE IMPORTANCE OF TRUST

Consider our credibility as managers. Because our message is sometimes incomplete, or if we are obviously uncomfortable delivering the news, our listeners sometimes feel we don't know what we are talking about. Once we lose credibility, people question our authority and whether we really care about them. Very quickly, we lose control.

Think about New York City's mayor, Rudolph Giuliani, during the weeks after the September 11 terrorist attack. He had the city's trust, he was credible to people in the rest of the United States, and he personified a dignified empathy.

These are the three things you want to make sure you impart when delivering bad news. First, that as the manager you are credible— meaning you have the knowledge and experience to deliver the message. Second, that you demonstrate empathy for the people who are impacted, caring about them, their well-being, and their future. Third, in your talk, you need to build trust, so people will continue to be responsible to you and the organization during this critical time.

Appreciating that we have to build empathy, credibility, and trust is not enough. We have to know what skills and behaviors to use to demonstrate those attributes when we speak to our colleagues. Let's take a look at the principle elements and then use an example to demonstrate how they are applied.

TIMELY DELIVERY OF NEWS

Rumor mills in corporate America are incredibly efficient. This efficiency has been enhanced through email, text messaging, and the cell phone. Employees can now deliver any message to each other within seconds. Sometimes they are even so thoughtful when they pass on their information that they begin the message with, "Don't tell anybody else, but . . ." Unfortunately, the "don't tell anybody" part gets dropped by the third person on the list and gets changed to, "You'd better tell everybody . . ." and implied in that is, "so we can prepare our retaliation strategy!"

No matter what, don't "sit" on the news. Get it out fast or it will find its way out on its own. The sooner you deliver the news yourself, the more you reduce the informal news flow, which is bound to be tainted in its delivery. By reducing that, you reduce anxiety and the desire for retaliation.

If possible, deliver your news in person to the total audience being impacted by the news. You want to be able to demonstrate credibility and empathy, and it is much easier to do that when they are seeing you live. Now, this can be a physical impossibility in our world of satellite home offices and cross-continental businesses. If you cannot deliver the message in person to everyone, have an "in person" meeting for your direct reports, and then use another media to reach the rest.

If "in person" is not possible, telephone conference calling is the next best method. This allows everyone to hear the same message and to ask the inevitable questions. Conference calls can be set up rather quickly and are cost efficient while allowing you to reach and involve everyone.

Email is and should be considered your last choice for delivering bad news. Although electronic mail messaging does have the advantage of being fast, it is an impersonal and one-way communication. Moreover, it can be altered, in transit.

The written word is a wonderful follow-up to the conference call or in-person interaction. It puts in writing any details that may have been difficult for the listeners to capture during the initial delivery of the news. Wherever possible, mail individual letters. This is the more personal approach, when you need to demonstrate empathy in these situations.

PREPARATION IS KEY

Speed is important, no question, but we can't shoot from the hip. Preparation is even more important when delivering bad news than good news. You know the recipients will hang on every word. Their careers may be impacted; their lives will be changed. What we say and how we say it is critical. Spend the time necessary planning what you will say both during the talk and in the question-and-answer session afterward. Think through what questions people are likely to ask and what answers you can share.

DEMONSTRATING LEADERSHIP
Donald Walton, a bestselling writer, speaker, and consultant on communications said,

> Those who become leaders are the ones who can best transmit their views, ideas, and enthusiasms to others. That is what a leader is.

I can't imagine a time when being a leader, pulling people together, is more important than when an organization is under duress. Although we are certainly troubled by the impact of the bad news, we must demonstrate our views, ideas, and enthusiasms—that there is something positive to come out of all this. Use your voice and body to enhance what you say. Volume, intonation, eye control, and physical skills become critically important. (Refer to Chapter 2, How to Stand Up and Speak as Well as You Think.)

HOPE AT THE END OF THE TUNNEL
The toughest part in hearing bad news is the sense of not knowing where the bottom is and what the future looks like. In delivering the bad news, it is very important that we lay out our own estimates and speak the truth when we do.

Tell employees where you understand the bottom to be. An example of this might be, "The hardest part of this change will be in the next few weeks, when you all determine whether you want to make this move or not," or "We expect to continue this moratorium on spending to the end of this quarter."

You can see how important it becomes that we also provide a positive outlook for the future. We cannot expect our employees to automatically see that ray of hope. It is very hard for anyone to see the future through the veil of change. Change is scary. If we can show our vision for that change, our hope for the future, we better equip our colleagues to help us reach that goal. An example of a vision might be, "This change will allow us to continue to compete in this market-place by focusing our resources," or "Once we move our services to a location that makes it easier for our customers to physically reach us, our sales should improve significantly."

THE IMPORTANCE OF TELLING THEM WHY

A logical question for listeners once they know what is happening is: *Why is it happening?* The tricky part is they don't really care about it from the corporate perspective; they care about it from their own perspective. If possible, make those personal and individual connections for them in what you say. These connections should include the value of making the changes as well as the negative consequences that may result.

For example, in a situation where a manager had to tell her employees that they were merging with the operations department and moving to offices 35 miles away, the value might be, "So our department can more easily utilize the resources of that department that we all need." The consequences might be, "Some of you will have a longer commute every day, and some will have a shorter commute. Some of you may decide to take a different job as a result of these changes."

DELIVERING BAD NEWS—THE FORMAT

Here, more than at any other time, your organizational format is critical so that people will be able to "hear" your message the way you intend. Below is the format for Delivering Bad News. This format works for the written follow-up as well.

BAD NEWS FORMAT

1. Set the stage
2. State the bad news
3. Give the rationale and consequences
4. Empathize
5. Look to the future
6. Answer questions

---

1. Set the stage. Give whatever background is necessary for other people to receive the news in context. This should be brief, mostly because they will stop listening if it isn't. There may be times when there is no need to give any background at all because they are all well aware of what is happening. Set the stage using phrases like, "In light of the new . . ." or "As you all know, we have had consultants helping us define our goals as an organization, which are to . . ."

2. State the bad news. The most important part here is to state the news directly. Hedging makes you come across as unsure of yourself; it negatively impacts your credibility. Don't withhold the critical information. State the bad news up front in the presentation. Don't build up to it.

3. Give the rationale. After you tell them what happened, the listeners will immediately want to know why. Give the rationale behind the bad news. The listeners will then want to know what the message means to them. State the consequences of the bad news.

4. Empathize. Throughout your message you need to express a supportive concern for the emotional impact of this situation. Empathy will also be demonstrated through the tone you use to deliver your message. Additionally, after you give the rationale and consequences, there needs to be verbal recognition on your part that you know this is hard for them. That's empathy.

5. Look to the future. Here the conversation turns an important corner. Now you're looking toward the future in a more positive light. That may mean suggesting actions that will preclude a replay of the bad news just delivered.

6. Answer questions and concerns. This is where much of your credibility will get developed. Anticipate questions your audience might ask. Develop answers ahead of time. Your preparation will signal to the listeners that you've done your homework and have given thorough consideration to their situation.

During events like this, there are often questions that don't have answers yet. Don't be afraid to say, "I don't know," and then give them a time when you can get the answers to them. Make sure you demonstrate that you are making note of those questions, so they believe you when you say that you will follow up. (See Chapter 5, How to Handle Audience Pressure.)

APPLYING THE PROCESS TO AN ACTUAL SPEECH

In 1969, something amazing happened in our world: Mankind actually landed and walked on the moon. A lot of planning and preparation went into making sure that experience was successful. But, as with all good leaders, President Richard Nixon also had to have a contingency plan. What if it was a disaster? What if we lost Neil Armstrong and Buzz Aldrin, either in space or on the moon? Part of that planning involved putting together a speech to "deliver the bad news" if things ended up that way. So a speechwriter for the president sent a memo to H. R. Haldeman on July 18, 1969, outlining a speech that could be used in the event of tragedy.

Let's look at that undelivered speech, attributed to William Safire, and see how the process of delivering bad news was incorporated into it:

Fate has ordained that the men who went to the moon to explore in peace will stay on the moon to rest in peace.

With this situation there is no need to set the stage. All the world was watching to see what would happen with the men on the moon.

These brave men, Neil Armstrong and Edwin Aldrin, know that there is no hope for their recovery. But they also know that there is hope for mankind in their sacrifice.

The bad news is stated directly: "There is no hope for their recovery." There was no hedging or building up to it, because the audience would want to know. Plus, if they know up front, they know how to listen to the rest of what is being said. The audience clearly has the context. In the sentence "They also know that there is hope for mankind," the speechwriter starts to initiate the idea that the future has a positive outlook.

These two men are laying down their lives in mankind's most noble goal: the search for truth and understanding.

They will be mourned by their families and friends; they
will be mourned by their nation; they will be mourned by
the people of the world; they will be mourned by a Mother
Earth that dared send two of her sons into the unknown.

Here, the speechwriter gives the rationale and consequences for what
is happening. The rationale is, "the search for truth and understanding . . . mankind's noble goal . . ." The consequences are that the
whole world will be mourning their loss. Empathy is displayed in the
statement, "Mother Earth that dared send two of her sons into the
unknown . . ."

In their exploration, they stirred the people of the world
to feel as one; in their sacrifice, they bind more tightly the
brotherhood of man.

Here the speechwriter again connects to the rationale and consequences
with his statement, "sacrifice . . . people to feel as one . . . bind more
tightly the brotherhood of man . . ."

In ancient days, men looked at stars and saw their heroes
in the constellations. In modern times, we do much the
same, but our heroes are epic men of flesh and blood.
Others will follow and surely find their way home.
Man's search will not be denied. But these men were the
first, and they will remain the foremost in our hearts.
For every human being who looks up at the moon in the
nights to come will know that there is some corner of
another world that is forever mankind.

To get people to look toward the future, the speechwriter connects the
future with something familiar from the past. Connecting with the
historically familiar makes it easier for people to feel that sense of
hope, and without hope it would be tough to move on. He does this
with his statement, ". . . in ancient days men looked at stars and saw
their heroes . . . in modern times . . . our heroes are epic men of flesh
and blood . . ." and then finishes it off with, "There is some corner of
another world that is forever mankind."

DEALING IN THE REALITY OF OUR EMOTION

One of the interesting things about this speech is that we can look at it now without our emotions blurring our thinking—because the event didn't happen. Emotion tends to cloud our ability to think rationally in difficult times. That will be true for the speaker and listeners alike when delivering bad news. We know people won't be happy to hear it. We may not even feel too good about it ourselves! Because of our own feelings, we not only need to plan our words, but ask someone who is not emotionally involved to review it for "tone."

THE LENGTH OF THE TALK

One of the attributes of this specific speech is it is brief—only 233 words. This is the same pattern you see at most press briefings. The actual speech is short. Most of the time for interaction is invested in answering follow-up questions.

In a corporate environment, the same pattern is effective. People are absorbing the news on their feet and immediately start to think of the impact on them. Their attention span, after you've delivered this emotional body blow, will be short. Tell them what you have to tell them, and then make it interactive with questions and answers. That pattern will move people toward looking to the future, to help make the necessary changes you are asking them to make.

KEY LEARNINGS FOR DELIVERING BAD NEWS

Do:

- Deliver the news as soon as possible, to preempt the rumor mill.
- Speak with energy and physical skills to support your message.
- Help your audience see the light at the end of the tunnel.
- Anticipate questions. Develop answers. Your credibility is on the line.

Don't:

- Hedge! Instead, be direct and to the point.

- Leave out the rationale. They might see the news through the wrong filter, which puts both the news and you in a negative light.

- Be afraid to say, "I don't know." Nothing erodes credibility faster than being caught in an untruth.

- Talk too long. Ten minutes maximum. Your audience will be feeling the force of the blow. Respect that.

12

HOW TO RUN A MEETING SO WELL YOUR PARTICIPANTS WILL APPLAUD

 ECENTLY, **I** WAS IN AN ANNUAL BUDGET MEETING for an organization that uses volunteers to manage its various committees. It turned out to be a classic example, in its way. There were about thirty people (half men, half women) there, half of whom knew each other. As they sat down, all were handed a three-ring binder filled with statistics and facts. We all flipped through the binders, but couldn't make much sense of the numbers and information that lay within, so we simply relaxed and waited to hear what the leaders of the organization would tell us.

About ten minutes after the published start time of the meeting, the person "in charge" cleared his throat rather loudly. The rest of us obediently stopped talking (some even closed the binders), since we recognized the clue to do so.

STARTING WITH A JOKE

The meeting chairman was new to his position, although he (and his bright red handlebar mustache) had been part of this organization for a long time. His mustache lifted as he began:

I heard a story the other day I would like to share with you. A not-so-bright woman dressed in a large fur coat recently got on an airplane and took a seat in first class. The flight attendant looked at her ticket and said gently, "Miss, I believe your seat is 22A. That is back there on the left next to a window."

The woman looked up and said, "I know. But I couldn't possibly sit back there because it would ruin my coat. There is not nearly enough room in those seats."

The flight attendant continued to explain. "I'm afraid I can't let you sit in this seat. It is assigned to someone else. I'll be happy to show you exactly where 22A is."

The woman continued to refuse to move, so, in frustration, the flight attendant went in to talk to the captain about the situation. The captain said, "I'll take care of it." He then walked over to the woman in the big fur coat and whispered in her ear.

Then, like magic, the woman stood up, said, "Oh. OK" and walked back to seat 22A.

The flight attendant was bewildered. She stood with her mouth open as she watched the woman go to seat 22A. Once that was taken care of she went back up to the captain and asked how he was able to get her to move?

The captain said, "Oh, that was easy. I just told her that first class was not going to Chicago.'"

The meeting chairman rested his mustache back on his lower lip, but the ends began to turn up as his smile grew from underneath. He waited for a roaring response from his funny story. But it didn't come. There were some half laughs, some chuckles, but mostly steely stares.

It was an ugly moment. Half the committee chairs were women, and they didn't laugh. Most of the others knew better than to laugh at a joke that put down half the population in the room.

THE INTERACTION BEGINS

As you might imagine, this meeting was now tension-filled. The chairman was uncomfortable. The committee chairpeople were uncomfortable, and many of the participants were darn right mad! How dare he? How dare he insult people as a way to show how warm, friendly, and funny he was? Most of the audience did not think he was funny. In fact, most people in that room no longer thought he was very smart. Credibility for our handle-barred friend was at its nadir, and no one in the room wanted to jump in and rescue him for fear they would be tarnished also.

Things did not get better. Our handle-barred friend started the official meeting content by saying, "Well, I don't really have anything to say. [We already guessed that of course!] Mr. Hawthorne, can you go over the budget guidelines?"

We didn't know who Mr. Hawthorne was until he started talking, because Handlebar had left out the part of the meeting where speakers are introduced. We looked and listened while Mr. Hawthorne told us how to get things approved, and what he needed from each of the committee chairs. Many of us flipped through the binder to find the location of the information that related to what Mr. Hawthorne was saying. Abruptly, it seemed, Mr. Hawthorne stopped talking. The room was silent.

Our handle-barred chairman started again. "Sean, why don't you explain the improvements that have been made in the last few months?"

Sean looked startled. "Well, I guess I could, but I hadn't really prepared anything to say."

Handlebar seemed surprised, perhaps annoyed. He retorted, "Well, you should always come prepared to present at my meetings, Sean, you know that." The rest of us didn't breathe. We felt sorry for Sean. That wasn't fair. If Handlebar hadn't prepared him, how would he know he was expected to speak? We gave encouraging smiles to Sean.

Again we searched through our binders to find the applicable pages. Sean was done. Silence.

MELANIE'S TURN

"Melanie is now going to tell you about how we have updated our website." We all looked to see which mouth would move next. We could narrow it down to only half of the audience, guessing Melanie was probably a woman. We were all praying Melanie was prepared to say something. We couldn't stand another Sean episode.

If Melanie wasn't prepared, she faked it well. Melanie talked for ten minutes or so. Unfortunately, we heard very little. We continued to try and find our way in the binders. For those of us who were new, we now knew the names and approximate responsibilities of four people in the room other than ourselves. Melanie stopped talking.

HANDLEBAR ASKS FOR QUESTIONS

Handlebar started again. "Well, that is all I can think of to discuss. Anyone have any questions?" There was silence.

One committee chair ventured, "How much notice do we have to give if we need more money for our committee?" It seemed like a reasonable question. After all, this was a budget meeting.

"Well, I am sure Mr. Hawthorne addressed that earlier, but I'll have him speak to that again if you weren't paying attention." Yikes! What a putdown. Then Mr. Hawthorne calmly answered the question.

"Any other questions?" asked Handlebar. Silence. No one wanted to risk another insult.

He asked another question. I had to hold back my gasp when I heard what it was. "Well, does anyone know any other good jokes then?" Another silence. Amazingly, the meeting was ending as badly as it had begun. No questions were asked. No comments were made. Just a handlebar-mustached man pointing to people in the room and asking them to talk about certain things.

AND THEN IT WAS OVER

We were done a full forty-five minutes before the scheduled end time. Lunch had been ordered, but it was only 11:15. There had never been introductions. Very few people in the room even knew each other, so only seven out of thirty stayed for lunch.

Now, let's analyze the format and impact of this meeting.

The first mistake wasn't the bad joke—it was the fact that no main speakers had been introduced, and meeting participants were not given a chance to introduce themselves. At the outset, everyone's identity remained hidden; we knew we were all chairpersons, but we didn't know who was who.

As for the joke, those who were angry about it were disenchanted and heard very little about the budget and processes they needed to follow. Those who were embarrassed by it also heard very little. The remaining few who thought the joke was funny (there are always a few) probably spent the whole meeting trying to figure out why everyone seemed so tense. So, they didn't get much out of the meeting either.

The Handlebar example is a horror story. But it is true. Each of you has probably lived through a similar experience. We hope it didn't happen in a meeting you ran.

A well-run meeting makes it possible to disseminate valuable information, share ideas, get consensus, and solve problems. It is also true that meetings provide visibility. Running an effective meeting provides the kind of visibility you want.

BUILDING SUCCESSFUL MEETINGS FROM THE START

Success in a meeting starts well before the meeting begins. It starts with the planning process. A few minutes of preparation can change the dynamics. You'll be more comfortable and the meeting stands a much better chance of being successful.

"Every meeting is a better meeting if, at the beginning of the meeting, we all know *why* we are meeting," says friend Kent Reilly, a successful consultant who has spent the last twenty years helping groups of people accomplish their meeting objectives.

It seems so simple, so why doesn't it happen? Maybe people assume that task force members would all know the objectives? Or that a training program would, of course, have participants who knew why they were there.

WHY ARE YOU CALLING THIS MEETING?
Why do we call meetings anyway? I guess it all got started with the old adage that two heads are better than one. Therefore three heads must be better than two, and so on.

The original thought is that when people are together, they can accomplish more than they might be able to alone. Is this always the case for your meetings? Can you accomplish more as a result of meeting?

The best place to start is by clarifying the purpose of the meeting. In its simplest form, the purpose answers the question, "What do I want people to do or think differently at the end of this time together?"

Take the Handlebar example. He had stated, in a letter to all of us, the purpose of the meeting—to review each committee's annual budget guidelines and answer questions the committee chairs had. Nicely done. Unfortunately, once the meeting began, he seemed to forget all that and didn't carry through on his well-stated purpose.

Clarifying the purpose will automatically force your meeting to be part of a solution to something, and that's better than people feeling that having to go to the meeting is just another sign that the organization itself is "not too organized."

WHAT DO YOU WANT PEOPLE TO DO DIFFERENTLY?

Purpose statements are active. They use verbs. They are moving in a direction. They help us accomplish the organization's goals. They are not a list of topics to cover. When the purpose is well-stated, it allows us, as meeting leaders, facilitators, or participants, to make sure our meeting helps us make progress.

Here are some sample purpose statements:

This meeting will address what our department's role will be in the restructured organization.

This meeting will help us to identify sales opportunities to develop proactively in the next quarter.

This meeting will help us plan individual business strategies, using the results of our recent customer survey.

This meeting is necessary to resolve outstanding issues from our last meeting.

The purpose of this meeting is self-education so that we can prepare ourselves for events that may impact us.

STICK TO THE PURPOSE

Once you've established the purpose, stick to it. That is the direction people prepare for. They will be better participants in your meeting if they are prepared. Your meeting will accomplish more, and you will build your credibility with the participants and within the organization.

Some meetings are meant to be informational; others will need to be more interactive. It is not always necessary to have a full-fledged, detailed agenda; some meetings are deliberately designed for the free-wheeling give-and-take of ideas. But when you begin, your very first words should describe the expected results of the meeting. This is your agenda and your end point. This gives you and other participants a way to measure the meeting's success. These expected results may be tangible, as in a written report; or intangible, such as new knowledge, motivation, or commitment.

If Handlebar had done this for our budget meeting, it might have sounded like this: "At the end of our time together, all committee chairs will understand their budget and procedures, know each other, know what their responsibilities are, and recognize who their resources are in the organization."

WHO SHOULD ATTEND?

Would you believe that at least 50 percent of all attendees come to a meeting not knowing why they are there? They look around and say to themselves, "Well, I know why John might be here, and Karen. And I can guess at why I might be here, though I don't know for sure. But why the heck would they invite Heather?" Not good. Often the person running the meeting looks around and thinks the same thing.

Whom should you invite? Invite those who can make a unique contribution to the meeting, or who have special expertise, or who carry official responsibility. Invite your decision makers. Also, since a meeting is a tool to help you accomplish something, you should invite a few of your own cheerleaders—those who can foster a positive attitude. People who can help you make progress—action people. You may want to invite those who would be responsible for implementing the decisions that are made in the meeting. Next steps will be easier to implement because these people will feel they have participated and been given an opportunity to provide some input.

Invite the right people and the meeting will "hum."

The number of people that attend a meeting should be carefully considered, because it does impact your success. If you are holding a problem-solving meeting, then as few as five people will do. Your job is to be sure it's the right five. Select them with an eye toward their ability to generate a diversity of ideas and their skill in troubleshooting. If your goal is to review or present information and you want interaction, you should limit the group size to fewer than thirty. Once a group goes beyond thirty, the attendees feel relatively unconnected and, therefore, unimportant. Because of that, there will be very little participation.

There is only one type of meeting that truly benefits from the masses attending. When your objective is to motivate or inspire, the bigger the audience, the better! (See Chapter 16.) A larger group creates a special energy in conjunction with the speaker that can magnify the impact of the meeting.

TELL THEM WHY

We need to tell people why they are invited, but also what their roles are to be in the meeting. We should also give attendees enough of a sense of what we expect to accomplish. They should be apprised of the attendance list so that they will pretty much understand why all the invitees are there. When everyone knows who will be there and why they are meeting, participants can focus on accomplishing the purpose of the meeting and not spend all their time there trying to figure out the political ramifications.

Aim to have no bench sitters in your meetings—each participant should expect to have a specific role—even your "cheerleaders."

Follow this principle: "Participation is the prerequisite to commitment." It will save you time and help you to achieve your meeting objectives.

MEETING LOGISTICS AND RULES

Additionally, you may need to assign logistical roles. Prepare your participants. Tell them if you expect them to speak on a particular topic. Ask someone to be the scribe or note-taker if necessary, or request that someone do a product demonstration. The key is using your resources; in a meeting, your resources are the people in the room with you!

I would strongly suggest sending out a meeting agenda beforehand, at least to the people who will be giving presentations. You will run a better meeting if you have worked out beforehand what the content is, how the content of the meeting will be discussed, and in what order. Announce who will be in attendance, the time, date, duration, and what preparation needs to be done before you get started.

Set ground rules for participation. Because not every meeting is the same, participants need to understand the expectations of them during this meeting. Develop them as a group, or prepare them ahead of time. The ground rules help guide the group toward your desired results. They become the commandments for participant behavior. They are a vehicle for the meeting chairperson to use to gently adjust behaviors back in a direction that works. Here are some sample ground rules:

- Only one person talks at a time.
- Avoid side conversations.
- Write down questions to ask *after* the speaker has finished.
- Take notes.
- Set aside last fifteen minutes for next steps and responsibilities.

Depending on the organization and the event, ground rules might be more formal. In very large groups, parliamentary rules can be extremely useful to maintain order and keep the participants on track. If you plan to have formal rules, it is a good idea to post them, or include them in a handout, as it allows you, the chairperson, to refer back to them for control.

HOW LONG?

The length of the meeting should always decrease as the number of your attendees increases. Let's look at the dynamics of this. The larger the audience, the less the members can actively participate in the meeting. They are mostly listening, and listening efficiency drops dramatically over time. So the rule is: With big audiences, hold short meetings.

Small "problem-solving" meetings can be longer. When the participants know why they are there, how they are expected to participate, and what the goal of the meeting is, longer meetings can actually accomplish more. Because problem-solving meetings are small, and, hence, more intimate, people stay involved and build off of each other's ideas.

Albert Einstein, a brilliant thinker by anyone's standards, says this about problem solving:

"The significant problems we face today cannot be resolved at the same level of thinking we were at when we created them."

In a problem-solving meeting, ideas need to evolve into solutions, and that takes time. This is time well-spent if the participants can come up with a satisfactory solution to a difficult issue. And, guess who gets credit for that solution? Yes, the participants, but also the talented meeting leader who ran the meeting so well!

WHAT ABOUT SUPPORT MATERIALS?

Use visuals whenever you can to manage the attention and understanding of the audience. People remember visuals. Visualize the problem, visualize the results, visualize your vision and goals of the meeting. Help people "see" what they are working on, and they are much more likely to remember it.

A FEW CAVEATS ABOUT HANDOUTS

Now that I've talked about the importance of visualization, let me issue a caution. Don't give the group a copy of your PowerPoint slides or a written report while trying to present an idea from the front of the room.

Why not? Because people are human, and humans who can read can't help but dig in immediately. If you put letters in front of them, they start sounding them out. Think about when you drive down a highway. You can't help but read the billboards. The same is true in a meeting. If you distribute written material, you will be up front talking about whatever you think is important, and they will be flipping through the pages of what you gave them and not paying the least bit of attention to you.

Now that is fine if you don't mind playing second fiddle to a handout. But the presenter should always be the star of the show. Only in an art gallery should the visuals get center stage. Never let it happen to you.

A HANDOUT RULE THAT WORKS

So here is the handout rule that works best. If you want your listeners to read something, give it to them well before the meeting, or give them time to read it without you or anyone else talking. You may also give them a copy of material (such as your PowerPoint slides) as they are leaving to complement whatever notes they took.

In professional situations the program chairman often asks for copies of the visuals from each speaker so that these materials can be duplicated and put into a folder for attendees. The idea is that the perfect way to take notes is to scribble them on the relevant handout page. Sometimes we lose that battle and have to supply the visuals. So what to do? Make sure your visuals are simple. Make sure they are pertinent, arresting, and interesting. Make sure they are eye-catching. Make sure they dramatize a point you want to make.

But make doubly sure the visuals don't tell the whole story. *You* tell the story. You are the creator of the news, not the visuals. The story must come from you, not the visuals. You are the source of life, of creativity, of ideas, of intelligence, of all that is interesting, not the visuals. The visuals can't hold a candle to you. The visuals should aid you—that is why they are called visual *aids*. They should help you make a thought clearer, more dramatic. But it's your thought, not the visuals, that should hold your audience's attention. Don't ever create visuals that contain the whole talk. You would be doing a disservice to the audience as well as to yourself.

Now—if you can create that kind of visual—one that doesn't compete with you—you can distribute it to the audience.

SCHEDULING THE MEETING

The facility can impact the climate of your meeting, which in turn impacts the level of success you have. Consider all the items that are important to you as a meeting participant, and assume they are important to others as well. Consider the size of the room, the acoustics, the ventilation, the lighting, and pick your site accordingly. People will rarely comment on the comfort of the room, but believe me, they will complain if it is not right. And they will complain while the meeting is going on, sotto voce. It will detract from your success.

WHEN TO MEET

Pick a time that doesn't predictably disrupt people's schedules. For example, you might steer away from 9 A.M. on Monday mornings, as well as any time after 3 P.M. on Friday afternoons. Also, keep in mind that the first hour or so after lunch, half of people's brains are in their stomach while they digest their food. And while a brain is in the stomach, it doesn't think very well.

If the meeting will occur during a conference that includes many social events, don't pick a time that's too close to the banquet luncheon, or might bleed into the trade show cocktail hour. Participants will have their minds on the party, not the issue at hand.

An effective way of picking a starting time is to start with the end time. Determine when your meeting has to be over, how long it will be, and from that calculate the starting time. That will help you control the length of the meeting and demonstrate your respect for the participants' other commitments.

Once the time is scheduled, make sure you abide by it. In your announcement, state that the meeting will start on time and end on time. And then, do your part. Start on the minute. It doesn't matter how many attendees are missing. Don't punish the punctual. Begin.

ALLOCATE TIME BY TOPICS
Do yourself a favor, a BIG favor! If it's a longer meeting—more than an hour—allocate time periods for each subject to be covered. Appoint a timekeeper. Introduce that person to the group and announce, "The timekeeper will notify us all when we get to the halfway point of each segment. He will also signal when there is only a half hour remaining, and fifteen minutes remaining."

Now, from the beginning, everyone will be aware that you understand the importance of time. This makes them confident the meeting won't drag on or run over. It also encourages the participants to be time-conscious; most will cooperate with you to move the agenda in line with the timing guidelines.

At the fifteen-minute point, bring the discussion to a close, as you've promised. Then, end the meeting like a professional. Nothing is so impressive as a meeting that is run well, accomplishes what it sets out to accomplish, and ends on time.

END THE MEETING LIKE A PRO
Make sure the meeting ends on time.

That doesn't mean that you should let time itself end the meeting. There is nothing worse than the meeting leader who has stated that the meeting will end at noon. The magic hour arrives. The meeting is in full swing, but our noble leader looks at his watch and says, "Oh my goodness, it's 12 o'clock. OK. Thanks everyone. I'll get back to you."

He stands up and shuffles papers. Everyone else stands and does the same. People begin to leave. There is a feeling of emptiness in the room. The participants are looking for a wrap up: agreements reached, next steps, a word of gratitude for the hard thinking that has taken place, a commitment to get back to them, something.

Ending on time is important. As a matter of fact, it's very important, because it reeks of professionalism. But a meeting should never end without these four things:

• A statement of heartfelt gratitude by the leader

• A summary of what has been accomplished

• Agreement on "next steps" and who's responsible

• An indication of what happens next

If you work at it, you can run the meeting so well your participants will applaud!

KEY LEARNINGS FOR RUNNING A MEETING WELL

Do:

• Start when you said you would. Don't punish the punctual.

• Establish the meeting's purpose. Communicate it to all. Let the purpose statement be your roadmap.

• Tell attendees what is expected of them and why. They are responsible, too.

• Time each segment. Appoint a timekeeper. Work within the timing guidelines.

• Conclude the meeting by wrapping up professionally so that participants know what they have accomplished and what they are expected to do next.

Don't:

- Open with a joke; they often fail. (And what a hole to dig out of!)
- Invite even one unnecessary person. Everyone should have a role and a responsibility.
- Hold a meeting without every attendee understanding his or her specific role and the meeting's purpose.
- End a meeting late. You blow it all if you run over the time scheduled for the meeting to end. Professionals finish on time.

13

HOW TO DISAGREE WITH YOUR BOSS WITHOUT GETTING FIRED

THIS TALE DATES BACK from when I first began working as an operations manager for Citibank. I was responsible for four of the operating units that supported the retail branch network. I was young, but I wasn't a kid.

The young part was in my operational experience. While I was "green" and had things to learn in the operations area, my previous work in marketing, sales, and sales management was valuable enough to qualify me for the new assignment. That's why they offered me the position.

MY NEW BOSS—HANK

My new boss was a man named Hank. I was somewhat awed by him as I took over my new job. He had started with the bank right out of school and had twenty-five years experience. My goodness, he had been with Citibank for almost as long as I had been alive! He seemed to know where to find the answer to every question, and he was thoroughly conversant with the various daily reports that tracked productivity, volume, mistakes, and so on. I was impressed . . . at first.

But it didn't last. After about one month on the job, Hank gave me an additional task: Create an incentive program that increased productivity. I was happy about this because it was an area in which I had a lot of experience—and I was eager to demonstrate my expertise.

But the happiness faded quickly. Hank gave me the task, then handed me a two-page outline that told me exactly what the program was and how to put it together. He then said, "I'd like to introduce the plan on Friday and begin on Monday. Let me know if there are any problems with that." It was instantly clear that this was an empty assignment. He was not looking for my input or ideas; He wanted me to implement, not think.

MY REACTION

I was deflated. Worse than that, I felt his design for the incentive program was all wrong and wouldn't work. His plan rewarded results, and these people didn't know what they needed to do to get those results. I wanted to design an incentive program around the behaviors that would make them effective. Hank wanted to start at the finish line, and the runners didn't know which way to run to get there! So I decided to tell him what I thought and, unfortunately, I didn't spend a lot of time strategizing what to say. I walked into Hank's office and said, "Your plan won't work, Hank."

He looked at me with a rather cold stare and said, "Well, of course it will work. We've done it this way for as long as I can remember."

"But you're rewarding the results instead of the behaviors, and that is strategically wrong with this audience. They don't know how to improve results on their own. I want to redesign it so that it will work. The existing program—the old way—won't work."

Hank looked at me with a hardened stare, "Just do it the way I said to do it." He walked away from me without saying another word.

To Hank's back I said, "I want to redesign it."

Without turning around, Hank said, "No."

NO ONE WAS HAPPY

I'm sure if Hank had to grade how he felt about me at that moment, I wouldn't have made the honor roll. Not good. A couple more of those situations and I might have never gotten a chance to develop my "operational knowledge"!

No question, Hank was unhappy, but he was not alone. I was *so* frustrated! I knew I was right. I knew Hank was wrong. It was as simple as that. But I didn't know how to get him to understand how right I was and how wrong he was.

I wish I could tell you that my brilliance saved me at this point. But it took me a little more time to figure out how to disagree with Hank and not get fired.

WHY START A WAR?

Let's step back now and analyze the dialogue that just took place.

My first comment to Hank was, "Your plan won't work." In just one sentence I managed to tell Hank that his twenty-five years of experience in this company were worth as much to me as flea powder. Being a red-blooded American boss, Hank felt attacked. And when people are attacked, emotions come into play.

With my first sentence, I had begun the war. Hank and I were both developing retaliation strategies. And everything we did at this point was colored by our emotions. No one could win. One of us would get our way (undoubtedly Hank) and, as Einstein once said so eloquently, "The war is won, but the peace is not." There would no longer be a neutral environment between us, no peace. And if that were to happen, guess who the big loser would be?

My explanation to help him understand my viewpoint had a good intention. But intent and effect are two different things. The effect was that I insulted him again, this time with details on why it was stupid (or he was stupid) to do it his way.

EMOTIONS UNDER THE INFLUENCE

George Thompson, in his insightful book *Verbal Judo,* offers a provocative thought on how our emotions influence our thinking. He says, "We all deal with people under the influence nearly every day. If it's not alcohol or drugs, it's frustration, fear, impatience, lack of self-worth, defensiveness, and a host of other influences."

Hank and I were now interacting with each other while under the influence—the influence of our egos, our frustration with each other, and our emotions.

My last salvo, which took place as Hank had effectively dismissed me, was, "I want to redesign it." Why should Hank even consider that idea? I had just told him his plans were stupid, implying that perhaps he was too. There was no way he could look at my plan with an open mind, or look at me without a sense of growing irritation.

A REENACTMENT—WHAT MIGHT HAVE BEEN

Let's re-create the story and look at how I should have handled this:

I am sitting in my office, and Hank comes in to talk about the productivity incentive program. "Here is what I want you to do with our incentive program." Hank hands me a two-page outline of what the incentive program had looked like in the past.

As I look down at the paper that was handed to me, Hank's deep cigarette-braised voice barrels out, "I'd like to introduce the program Friday and begin on Monday. Let me know if there are any problems with that." Hank heads back to his office.

WHAT DO I DO?

I try to think clearly enough to develop a plan. I start thinking about what he said and why he acted that way. I have to ignore my anger and quiet my thumping heart; I need to think from his perspective. If I understand what he likes most about his plan, I can figure out how to present my own recommendations in a way that might intrigue him, maybe even excite him. But to do that, I realize, I really need more information. I need to ask questions and get Hank to talk.

HOW TO GET THE BOSS TO LISTEN

When emotional, always begin with questions, not statements. Getting the boss to listen to you when you have a disagreement requires tact and a defined strategy. Here is a format to use when you need to have a productive two-way conversation:

THE DISAGREEMENT FORMAT

1. Develop your understanding.
2. Paraphrase your understanding.
3. Tie your idea to the boss's needs.
4. Ask an open-ended question.
5. Thank your boss!

HERE'S HOW THE STRATEGY MIGHT HAVE WORKED FOR ME:

1. Ask key questions to develop your understanding.
I go into Hank's office with a pad of paper and pen. I ask Hank if it would be OK if I asked him a few questions to help me understand more fully his perspective on the incentive plan.

He smiles and says, "Sure."

His smile is effortless; mine, a bit forced, but it's there. I continue, "What are the results you are looking to achieve with this incentive plan?"

This question provides a valuable focus: The answer will tell me what my boss's real objectives are.

Hank obliges by saying, "Well, the incentives help motivate the staff at a key time—when our work volume is high. So we kill two birds with one stone. We increase productivity at a time when we need it most."

Then I ask:

"What do you like most about the current program?"

This question is also very important. Hank has been doing things his way for decades. I need to find out why he values the method and what his favorite parts of the program are.

Hank has to think for a minute on this one. "It helps manage the budget. I know this time of year is going to be a period when we are more heavily staffed. The incentive program doesn't cost us nearly as much as it seems to when you factor in the increase in productivity. We actually hire less staff than we would have to otherwise."

My follow-up question for Hank is:

"What do you like least about the program?"

Hank laughs. (My stomach is still in knots, but he laughed! I must be doing something right.) "Well, that's an easy question. It's the timeliness of tracking results, because we don't get the results until two weeks later. That makes it a little less effective as a motivator. People have to wait to see if they've 'won.'"

The answer to this question is extremely valuable if the goal is to change my boss's mind. Here he has just handed me the one part of his time-tested, favorite program that even he feels could use some improvement. This is the "in"—the wedge to open his mind to a new idea.

2. Paraphase your understanding of what the boss has told you.
During your information-gathering efforts, it will help a great deal if you paraphrase your understanding of what your boss is trying to accomplish. Ask a closed question—one that requires a "yes" or "no" response—to verify that understanding. This demonstrates your listening ability and your respect for your boss's opinions. So, if I can show that I respect his opinions, Hank is more likely to respect mine:

"So Hank, if I understood you correctly, you are looking for the incentive program to increase productivity and manage your employment expenses. Additionally you are looking to get program results on a timelier basis, so they could be an even more effective motivator. Is that correct?"

Hank looks pleased. "That is exactly what I want."

3. Tie your idea to what you've learned about the boss's needs and concerns.
We've talked about the "tie back" that links the words of a presentation to your key point when you are speaking to an audience. In this case, when the audience is your boss, the better strategy is to "tie back" your key point to something he or she wants to hear—a reiteration of the desired program result, chief value, or main concern. By doing this, you allow your boss to see the value of your idea through his or her own lens.

Here, I take a deep breath. "Well, I think I know what you are looking for, Hank. I'm confident that I can come up with a way to do this—develop a plan that builds on our existing program with even greater productivity and more timely results. I will need a few days to do that. If it is OK with you, I'd like to do some work on this immediately and come to you Friday with a plan to meet your objectives."

4. Ask an open question to get the boss's reaction.
This is how you avoid the deadly word "no" and keep your boss feeling very much in charge of the decision, while you are still managing the interaction. So I say, "What do you think, Hank?" I smile confidently and hold my breath waiting for his reply.

Hank looks at me and doesn't say anything for a few moments. "I guess that would be OK. But no later than Friday. I want to get started because our peak volume period is sneaking up on us very quickly!"

Now I can smile, and the smile is real. "No problem, Hank. Friday it is."

5. Thank your boss for listening and considering your input.
Always remember to thank your boss for agreeing to talk with you. (You want that behavior to continue!) Here's my new parting line:

"Thank you, Hank, for the additional clarification and for letting me work on an even better program. You won't be disappointed."

Let's summarize what has happened in this "Right Way" scenario, using the "disagree with your boss and not get fired" principles. I have demonstrated my respect for my boss and maintained my integrity. In fact, I have even enhanced it. If my program works (which I know it will), I begin to build a track record of success and a level of trust with Hank.

The right way to disagree is to replace any pattern of confrontation with a strategy that builds your credibility while improving your working relationship.

EVERYONE'S GOAL—TO INCREASE SALES
Here is another example, but the circumstance is slightly different. The constant is that the subordinate and the boss disagree. I'll change the names to protect the innocent, but we'll still see how the principles apply.

The company is a large insurance organization. Adrian is the senior vice president of human resources, and John reports to him as the vice president of training. Adrian, the boss, does not have sales experience. His background is in human resources. John came up through sales, spent some time in sales management, and, through a twist of fate, ended up running the training organization.

The company is committed to increasing its share of market. To do so, it must find ways to increase sales. Human resources has to get involved because the company suffers from high employee turnover in sales. Management believes the sales force is not generating and closing sales opportunities as well as they should. John and Adrian need to have a discussion about how to use a training initiative to help the sales force become more productive.

John can handle the situation quite well: He is very sensitive to Adrian and where he is coming from. He disagrees with Adrian—nothing uncommon there. It's part of life. But the way he will reduce the friction in the dialogue is uncommon and artful.

The setting is this: John is waiting in the conference room when Adrian walks in with his "Coffee Grande" cup. This is probably his third this morning, since it's 8:30 and he usually gets in around 6 A.M. His shining silver hair, impeccable dress, and melodic voice make you think he might have had an opportunity on Broadway had he not gotten into the insurance business.

John is in the room already. He arrived a few minutes early (because he always does) to lay out the information he wants to go over with Adrian. Although John is sitting, it is immediately obvious that he'd make a better football player than a jockey. He is 6' 3" and also cuts an imposing figure across a conference table.

Adrian chimes, "Well, good to see you here ready and early, John. We have a lot to discuss and as usual, not enough time to do it justice."

John, a man of fewer words than Adrian says, "I'm ready."

JOHN ASKS QUESTIONS TO DEVELOP HIS UNDERSTANDING

John continues, "I'm prepared to talk about my ideas on the topic with you, Adrian, and I'm sure you have some thoughts as well. If you would share your thoughts first, I think it will help us use our time together most productively."

Adrian, in a voice slightly too loud to be talking to one person, says, "Our people are just not good in front of the clients. They need some help with their selling skills."

John is shocked. He can't believe that Adrian didn't mention prospecting abilities. In his view, presentation skills are of little value if the company can't find new clients in the first place. But he does manage to choke out a useful phrase that will buy him some thinking time: "Say a little more about your thoughts on that, Adrian."

Adrian, happy to have the airtime, says, "Sure. I am not sure our salespeople know how to sell, what questions to ask, or what the needs of our customers are. I want them in front of the customers having the skills necessary to connect their offer of products to what the customer needs."

JOHN PARAPHRASES HIS UNDERSTANDING

Though John feels this comment is an insult to his sales staff, he will go ahead to paraphrase his understanding of what Adrian was really trying to say. So he asks a closed question to verify that understanding:

"So, if I understand you correctly, you want them in front of the customer as much as possible, and when they get in front of the customer, you want them to have the skills necessary to sell our products and services. Is that correct?"

Adrian responds back using his typical enthusiasm, "Yes, in front of the customer and skilled."

JOHN TIES HIS IDEA TO THE BOSS'S NEEDS

John takes a deep breath and begins, "I agree. I want them in front of the customer as much as possible and skillful in their process."

Then he gracefully attaches his idea to Adrian's, so that the two ideas mesh: "In order to do that, we also want to consider helping them understand what skills will help them get in the door more often."

It works. Adrian looks at John and says, "Yes that sounds like a very good idea. You know my job depends on the success of this initiative, and because of that, yours does as well."

"Yes, I understand," John responds. "That is why I would suggest that we look at this as a two-stage process. First, develop skills that will help our salespeople get in the door more often. And, second, once they get there . . . teach them skills that will connect their offer of products to what the customer needs. I believe that two-pronged approach will afford us the highest level of success."

JOHN ASKS AN OPEN-ENDED QUESTION TO GAUGE REACTION
"How does that sound, Adrian?"

"OK," said Adrian. "Go ahead and start contacting vendors so we can begin to have an impact as soon as possible."

JOHN THANKS HIS BOSS FOR LISTENING
"Thank you, Adrian, for your advice and approval on this. I'll begin the vendor selection process immediately."

John was successful using the "disagree and don't get fired" principles. He was able to keep Adrian "open" to hearing his ideas by using the principles. Now I can't promise that you will always be as successful as John was in convincing your boss, but the thought of firing you will be the furthest thing from your boss's mind. And since you are helping your boss get pet projects accomplished in such a collaborative way, he might wind up looking at you and thinking: "Promotion!"

KEY LEARNINGS ON HOW TO DISAGREE WITH YOUR BOSS AND NOT GET FIRED

Do:

- Use words like "suggest" when dialoguing with your boss. No boss bristles at a suggestion. And it's easier to embrace one because there's no pressure.

- Be enthusiastic when you present your ideas. If you don't like them, why should anyone else?

- Appreciate what is good about your boss's perspective. Use the tie back technique. Build on what you both agree on and go forward together.

Don't:

- Open the meeting with your idea. The boss wants to talk. Let the boss talk. Then marry your solution to what he or she is trying to do. That way you both win, and the boss thinks you're terrific.

- Use the words, "but," "although," or "however," in your communication. These words often act as erasers that negate what precedes them. If you are tentative in your dialogue, you're giving your boss another good reason not to listen to you.

- Think you can be a winner without the boss on your side. When we go it alone, we often die alone.

- Tell your boss he or she is wrong. Misinformed, maybe, but not wrong. If you press too hard on that front, you're gone.

14

HOW TO PERSUADE THROUGH A TALK

ACK WELCH, THE FORMER CHAIRMAN of General Electric, in
his book, *Straight From the Gut,* writes about never wanting
to see a planning book before someone presented it. He said,
"To me the value of these sessions wasn't in the book . . . I
needed to see the business leaders' body language and the
passion they poured into their arguments."

He went on to say, "Making initiatives successful is all about
focus and passionate commitment."

Toward the end of the book, he discusses passion specifically: "Whenever I go to Crotonville and ask a class what qualities define an 'A' player, it always made me happiest to see the first hand go up and say, 'Passion.' For me intensity covers a lot of sins. If there is one characteristic all winners share, it's that they care more than anyone else."

Winners show they care; they don't hold back. We gravitate to these leaders because they appear so committed to their beliefs. Their commitment makes it easier for us to follow their lead, to "jump on board" their ship.

A LEAP OF FAITH

This jump is a leap of faith. We usually don't "leap" unless the leader leaps first. Our leader has to show us that he or she is assuming risk and that the cause is worth it. The leader has to passionately want us to join in or join up, to be with him or her "on the other side."

How does that apply to you if you want to persuade through a talk? You'll probably not be successful through intellectual argument alone. You'll have to show that you believe, that you care, that you're totally committed. You must share feelings, emotions, beliefs, and convictions.

COMMENTS YOU LIKE TO HEAR

Consider for a moment what kind of comments you like to hear after you make a presentation. You would probably be pleased to hear statements like these:

"Your argument was tightly focused."

Or, "You really had that one buttoned up."

Or, "Your presentation was tight, well prepared."

Or, "You really nailed that presentation."

Or, "You sure put forth a disciplined argument."

Those comments are businesslike. They feel OK.

You might be less comfortable with these:

"You sure put a lot of feeling into that presentation."

Or, "You took your listeners on an emotional roller coaster with that presentation."

These comments sound emotional. In business, most of us don't like to be thought of as emotional. Yet, if you are going to be successful in persuading an audience, you must expose your heart as well as your mind. That's hard for most of us to do. We feel vulnerable. And, indeed, we are.

RISKS INVOLVED

There are some risks involved here. If our goal is to persuade, we have to commit ourselves to a new world. It's a world where feelings come to the forefront. To be successful in persuading or motivating an audience, you must believe. And you must show that you believe. You need to be committed to the subject, committed to the audience, committed to the result. No trap door. No exit strategy. You are moving forward, and you want your listeners to get swept up by your enthusiasm for the subject or the project: "If you feel so strongly, it must be a good idea."

IF YOU DO IT WELL

If you communicate your passion well, the audience will tune in to you. They won't look at you as just another speaker up there. They will identify with you in an almost evangelical way. They will even allow you a minor imperfection in your argument so long as you are perfect in your belief. They will overlook an occasional garbled syntax or even a grammatical mistake. But if your talk is void of emotion, it will miss its mark. The audience will sense a lost chord. They will see that your heart is not in it. They will feel hollowness, and all will be lost.

If that is not daunting enough, there is another thing the audience will be assessing as you speak—and that is your character. Here is a beautiful statement by Ralph Waldo Emerson, one of the great minds our country has produced:

> *What you are thunders so*
> *that I cannot hear*
> *what you say.*

We should keep that in mind whenever we speak to an audience, but especially when our purpose is to motivate. Dale Carnegie once said, "Don't be worried about getting hold of the subject; just be sure the subject gets hold of you."

THE POWER OF PASSION IN SPEECH

The most important element in a talk to persuade is your belief in the "rightness" of the course you are asking the audience to take. The most persuasive evidence used in support of your belief is a human-interest story. A great story enables you to speak your mind and bare your soul.

Let me share a story with you: how a masterful talk to motivate and persuade saved the day.

A BIG SALE—THE MARINE CORPS

Back in the early days of Communispond, we were a subsidiary of J. Walter Thompson (JWT), and a pretty small subsidiary at that, with only ten employees. JWT was the world's largest advertising agency and proud of it. The United States Marine Corps was one of its accounts. We at Communispond capitalized on this relationship to land our biggest sale ever, a three-year contract to train all Marine Corps recruiters in speaker skills.

We did this work at the Marine Corps recruiter school in San Diego. It's a six-week school that is run six times a year, covering all the subject matter the recruiter needs in order to carry out his or her responsibilities. Speaker training is taught for two days in each six-week cycle.

Nine hundred applicants for recruiter training were selected each year on a quota basis from each of six regions. They were staff sergeants and up. Requirements were three years of high school, four years of service time, and a recommendation from their commanding officer. The "tour" in this billet was two years and was considered a prestigious appointment.

The recruiter school was tough and demanding. Once a recruiter graduated, he or she was assigned to a recruiting office in any one of a hundred or more locations, usually in a highly populated area. Recruiters had to find prospects, excite them about a career in the Corps, and persuade them to sign up.

Where to find them? High schools, of course. How to excite them? By giving talks to the senior class. That's why speaker training was so important. The Marine Corps needed recruiters, and the recruiters needed speaker training.

A BUDGET CHALLENGE

Seven months into our program, we received a letter from General Schultz, the head of Marine Corps Recruiting, saying the Corps was eliminating speaker training for the last four months of the year. Just like that, they were going to cut one-third of our business! In the letter, we were also afforded the opportunity "to plead your case if you disagree with the actions we are taking."

Sure, we'd plead our case, but it was obviously perfunctory. The business was gone. It was a "budget thing" for the Marine Corps. Overall they had to cut millions of dollars. Virtually all suppliers were cut. We were part of it—a very small part, from their vantage point. Huge from ours.

Prior to the dreaded meeting, three of us at Communispond met to discuss what we might present. The three were Charlie Windhorst, my partner and cofounder of the company, Jim McGuirk, the account manager who was responsible for the account, and myself. We talked and argued and tried to work out a strategy to save the business.

Our dilemma was real. Charlie phrased it best: "How do you win an argument with the United States government when they have the money, the authority, and the Marine Corps on their side?"

WHO MAKES THE TRIP?

One thing we agreed on was that Jim McGuirk and I would both make the trip. I would go because I was the president, and the letter asked for my presence. Jim would accompany me because he was the main person on the account and knew it inside out. He was our man who welcomed each group of 175 candidates to the San Diego recruiter school on behalf of Communispond Speaker Training. In the course of eight months, he had addressed some six hundred recruiter school attendees and personally spent two days teaching most of them. In addition, he was our number-one instructor.

Jim was New Jersey born and about thirty-five years old. He had somehow never spent time in the military. His hair was a little too long for the business community, much less the Marine Corps. In that era, he looked sort of like a hippie. If you went to central casting to select a person to handle the Marine Corps account, you wouldn't pick Jim McGuirk. But he was as smart as he could be and a magnificent instructor. And he cared. Oh my, how he cared.

THE MEETING

Jim and I were ushered into a fairly large conference room. Sitting around the table were eleven marines, all in uniform.

Here was the assemblage:

- General Brown, Chief of Staff, the third ranking Marine Corps officer after the commandant and the assistant commandant
- General Schultz, head of Marine Corps Recruiting
- Four full colonels (these four gentlemen had some aspect of responsibility for recruitment and budgeting)
- Two lieutenant colonels (members of General Brown's staff)
- Lt. Colonel C. D. Silard Jr., head of recruitment advertising
- Two majors, including Major Pete Rowe, the Marine Corps liaison with J. Walter Thompson advertising agency

On our side of the table were Jim McGuirk and me. "Holy cow," I thought, "that's thirteen people in one room for one rather perfunctory meeting."

We went through the normal small talk first. I shook hands with each of them. I always do that when I teach a Communispond program, and I thought it was probably a good idea here as well. One thing I've learned is that if an instructor shakes hands with a participant before the program, that person will more likely be an advocate rather than a problem. I'm sure politicians feel the same way.

There was another reason. Neither Jim nor I had ever shaken the hand of a general before. We were like anyone else. We were awed by their crisp uniforms, by the gold braid on their hats, and by the stars on their shoulders. And we were respectful of those officers who had achieved so much.

But we had a job to do. Our company was small, only ten people. All ten depended upon Communispond for their income. And those Marine Corps officers were intent on taking a large part of it away from us. At least that's the way we looked at it.

THE COLONEL OPENS

One of the colonels opened the proceedings by outlining the framework in which this meeting was being held:

"The United States government has conducted a budget review, as it always does at this time of year, and found that it was running above budget. It is requiring all branches of the military to identify areas where proposed activity could be postponed or cancelled. It has asked the Marine Corps to "find" twenty-seven million dollars. The Communispond speaker training has been earmarked as a contributor to this saving. Our letter to you, Mr. Daley, explained all this. You have been offered the opportunity to respond to our letter of intent and give your perspective on our planned action."

I thought to myself, "This colonel is obviously a budget man. Jim and I don't have a chance to turn this around." Nonetheless, I began.

OUR PRESENTATION

I showed some statistics. We had trained 613 recruiter candidates thus far. The students rated each course in the five-week school. I presented the ratings. The numbers were awesome. I felt immense pride in what Jim and our other instructors had accomplished.

Overall rating of speaker training on a 5.0 scale	4.8
Rating of our Communispond instructors	4.9
Importance of speaker training	4./
Average rating for all other subjects covered in the six-week recruiter school	3.9
Highest rating for any subject other than speaker training in the six-week school	4.4

The eleven Marine Corps officers around the table had to be impressed. But they didn't show it.

I read samples of the verbatim evaluations written by the students. They were overwhelmingly positive. They loved the training. They wanted more, not less. They said it was the best feature of recruiter school.

I read out loud some of the evaluations of speaker training written by the staff of the San Diego school. They taught all subject matter in the school except for speaker training, but there was no professional jealousy. They were equally positive and supportive of what we had done.

I ended by saying that we felt the impact of the six-week school would be diminished if the budget cut were maintained. I asked that the order be rescinded and that speaker training be reinstated. I sat down, knowing that I had gone through the motions but that my presentation wasn't going to change any minds.

THE GENERAL RESPONDS
General Schultz reinforced that perspective when he said, "Thank you, Kevin, for your informative review. We are pleased with the work you and your people have done for the Marine Corps and certainly hope that, in the future, you will have the opportunity to continue your work with the recruiter school in San Diego. I must emphasize the point that the action we are taking is brought about by budget constraints alone. It is not a reflection on you or your company."

Then he looked around the table and asked, "Does anyone else have something to say on this subject?" At that point I knew it was over. We had made a darn good case for our side, but they were on a mission to reduce expenditures and they had to remain firm.

The general waited a full ten seconds with no response. He rose to his feet, obviously intent on ending the meeting and said, "Very well then . . . "

JIM McGUIRK SPEAKS
But he was interrupted by Jim McGuirk, who stood up and said, "General Schultz, if you will allow me, I do have something to say." General Schultz nodded and sat back down. (I was surprised that Jim was speaking because we hadn't talked about this). Jim began:

> I've worked with more than six hundred Marine Corps recruiter candidates in the past eight months. As you know, they each spend two days learning how to speak to an audience on behalf of the Marine Corps. They learn how to handle a sometimes-restless audience of high school seniors. They learn to be interesting, sometimes even entertaining. They learn how to present the Marine Corps as an exciting career with immense opportunity.
>
> They also learn how to look the father of a seventeen-year-old in the eye and say, "The Marine Corps is an institution, larger

than most of the major corporations in the country. The career opportunities for your son (or daughter) are just as varied. We will help your child discover what talent he has. We'll teach the skills that she needs. They'll learn a trade or an occupation. They will learn teamwork, self-discipline, loyalty to their fellow marines, love of country, and faithfulness to its ideals. It's a great life if he or she wants it and if he or she qualifies."

The recruiters have to learn to tell that story credibly. That's our job. We teach them to communicate the Marine Corps story, to tell it well, to tell it persuasively, to be better recruiters.

THE STORY
Jim continued:

But we do so much more. Let me tell you a story. I had one young lad in my class. His name was Steve, twenty-four years old, with four years in the Corps. Steve was a decorated Vietnam hero. He had a bull neck and a high and tight haircut. And he wore the uniform well, chest out, chin up. You just looked at him and you could tell he was proud to be a marine.

But he was afraid to stand and speak in front of the group. He trembled. He shook. The words were almost inaudible. I worked extra hard with Steve, pushing, cajoling, coaching him, through each of the eleven talks that he gave in the training. He had so much potential. And he got better, and better, and better.

At the end of the two days he came up to me and said,

"Sir, can I say something to you?"

I said, "Of course, Steve."

He said, "Sir, these have been the finest two days of my life." He paused for a moment as though to gather his thoughts. "Before this school, I've always been terrified of an audience. I couldn't do it. I've been ashamed, but I felt helpless."

Steve finished by saying, "Today, I finally feel like a man. I thank you for that."

> I shook his hand, and my eyes filled with tears. Top Teeter, a Master Gunnery Sergeant on the staff, was with us at the time, and he said, "Jim, you are not supposed to cry in front of marines." He was laughing as he said it, but he had tear marks on his face, too.

I looked at the eleven Marine Corps officers listening to Jim. They were rapt, still, hardly breathing. Jim went on:

> I'm not apologizing for my tears. I had just witnessed a miracle. I had watched a twenty-four-year-old marine overcome a fear that had tied him in knots his entire life. I saw a decorated war hero become a better man, a better marine.
>
> And that's what our speaker training is all about. It's about young men and women discovering themselves, discovering the potential and the power that resides in them. It's seeing a young boy become a man right before your eyes. It's seeing a United States Marine stand taller because she knows she can face any audience and handle herself well.
>
> And that's the risk you have to weigh as you consider eliminating this training. If you take it away, how do you replace this life-defining experience? Where else can your recruiters get it? Where else can they go? They look to you to make the decisions that are best for the Marine Corps and best for them.
>
> You have to save money, you've told us that. Your overall need is twenty-seven million dollars. And you are looking to save a small portion of it by canceling speaker training. I understand your need.

A PASSIONATE PLEA

Jim concluded with:

> But I implore you to look for it where the damage is not so great. Don't save it where it hurts these young men and young

women the most. Don't save money at the expense of their self-esteem. Don't take away what Steve called, "the two finest days of my life." Don't take away the training that gives them courage to do their jobs as recruiters.

So where do you find the money you are trying to save?

Jim asked this rhetorical question softly, as though he were talking to himself. Then he paused, looked at General Brown, and said in steadily increasing volume:

Sell a tank.

Sell a tank.

Sell a tank!

Then he said his final sentence very softly:

But don't deprive these fine young men and women of the opportunity to become stronger, more confident, better marines than they were before.

Jim sat down. Everyone was sitting. There was only silence. Then General Brown, the senior officer in the room, stood up and walked toward Jim and me. He was smiling. He had his hand out. Since I was the president of Communispond, I assumed he was reaching for me. So I put my hand out, but he walked right by me. It was Jim's hand he clasped, and he shook it like an old friend.

GENERAL BROWN RESPONDS

Then he said in a strong voice, which could be heard by all:

"Jim, I am deeply moved by your presentation. What you have shared with us captures the true spirit and heritage of the Marine Corps.

"As an organization, we challenge our men and women to constantly reach for new levels of excellence. We are not satisfied with the commonplace. Our recruiting slogan says, 'The Proud, The Few, The Marines.' We must never forget that the growth and development of our personnel is what makes the Corps the elite branch that it is.

"We will meet and discuss your presentation."

Then he turned to me and said, "Kevin, you will hear from us within a week. The meeting is adjourned."

Jim and I kept our game faces on until we found an empty room. Then we hugged one another and said, "We've got a chance. Believe it or not, we've got a chance!"

THE RESULTS

On the following Monday we received a letter from General Schultz reinstating the remainder of our speaker training schedule. I read the letter out loud to the entire office. We whooped and hollered. Since when did the United States government, or the United States Marine Corps, ever change its mind?

We analyzed what had happened. Facts and statistics had not done the job. Only Jim McGuirk's passion could break through their wall of resistance. He persuaded them.

Is there a lesson in this experience? Yes, there is. Never underestimate the power of intensity, the power of a passionate appeal, the power of a presenter's total commitment to his cause—the power of a great story.

You may worry that you might overdo this, go to far, show too much passion. Are there such times? The answer is yes, but not when selling an idea or persuading a group. It is true that passion can work to your disadvantage when you are being critiqued or criticized. If you find yourself deliberately put on the defensive, then you are probably better off being cool and calculating in your demeanor.

But when you are trying to generate excitement inside your listeners, you had better pump up your own excitement so that they can tell you are holding nothing back. Here is another quote from Ralph Waldo Emerson: "Every great movement in the annals of history is a triumph of enthusiasm." Passion and enthusiasm are closely related.

They contributed mightily to Jim McGuirk's triumph. They will do the same for you—so long as you don't hold back.

KEY LEARNINGS FOR DELIVERING A TALK TO PERSUADE

Do:

- Find a human-interest story that moves you greatly. Then tell it so true to life that your audience is moved the same way you are.
- Appeal to the nobler motives of the audience.
- Dramatize! Share your passion, your feelings, your commitment, your emotions. Let it all hang out. Hold nothing back.
- Be clear in what you want your listeners to do.

Don't:

- Rely on an intellectual argument alone. The issue here is passion, not rules.
- Worry about being vulnerable. Your vulnerability is central to the power of the talk.
- Hold back. This talk will be successful if you give everything you've got to make it so.
- Remain seated. Sitting drains you of power. Stand straight and tall and speak from the heart!

15

HOW TO EMCEE AN EVENT, INTRODUCE SPEAKERS, AND PRESENT AWARDS

OU HAVE BEEN ACCEPTED AS A LEADER in your company or your community. You have been asked to serve as a program chair for a dinner or master of ceremonies (otherwise known as MC, or emcee) for a more lavish event. It's quite an honor. It means you are known by the audience and respected by the people putting the event together. If you do it well, you are admired anew and you grow in stature within your company and with all those in attendance.

YOUR FIRST RESPONSIBILITY—TO OPEN THE EVENT

Your first responsibility is, of course, to open the event, to welcome everyone. Usually you will do this from a platform or a stage. How you do it creates the climate for the meeting. You either lift the audience and build anticipation, or you bore them and create apathy. As such, you are the catalyst. You carry the audience on your shoulders. At this point, they are a clean slate. You are the artist who determines what is painted there.

Many years ago, there was a great speaker named Percy Whiting. He would always greet the audience by asking in a booming, microphone-aided voice, "Can you hear me in the back over there?" while pointing to the far right corner. A few brave members of the audience in that corner would shout back, "Yes, we can hear you!"

Percy would then turn and gesture to the far left corner while booming, "Can you hear me in the back over there?" The answer would come back, "Yes we can!" Then Percy would say at the same high volume level and with his arms outstretched, "Well, then, let's begin!"

YOU ARE THE FOCAL POINT
Here's what Percy Whiting accomplished by opening in that way:

* He became the focal point. All side conversations ceased. He got everyone's attention and brought the group to order.
* He achieved audience interaction. Members of the audience actually spoke out loud. Amazing!
* He created excitement. The anticipation level started off on a high.

That was what he wanted to accomplish. That was his purpose. Yet it all seemed so natural as far as the audience was concerned. It was fun, and it stirred everyone to attention.

IDENTIFY KEY PEOPLE IN THE GROUP
In the crowd, of course, will be significant people within your organization. They need to be recognized for any number of reasons—if nothing else, they have marquee value with the audience, and their

noted attendance will lend prestige to the event. Let's use an example. We'll assume that you are the program chairman for a fund-raising event for your local YMCA. There are seven hundred people present. Once you have opened the session and welcomed those in attendance, you need to give ample recognition to the officers, the directors, and the people who were responsible for putting the event together.

Do it individually for the key people. Decide with them beforehand if they will stand when their names are mentioned. Make sure you know how to pronounce their names. If you muff an important name, you're a dead man—or woman. And it feels bad, too. If there is a difficult name, ask its owner how it's pronounced. Then say it back to them at least three times. Then write it phonetically in your notes. Then say it five times to yourself before your moment of truth.

PROVIDE THE COMMON BOND

Next, tell the audience "why we are all here." This critical opening statement tells the crowd why your prominent panel of speakers is taking the time to be present and offers a connecting common thread that brings the speakers and the entire audience together. You need to find this thread, state it, and connect everyone.

AN EXAMPLE OF AN OPENING

We are here tonight because the "Y" is, in some way, important to each of us. Certainly many of us use the Y regularly as an adult fitness facility. And it's the best and most affordable one in town. But that's not where the great Y legacy comes from. It comes from what it has done for kids. Probably 75 percent of you folks in this room can remember a time when you were a kid and the Y made a positive difference in your life.

And though the Y has programs for every age group, kids are what we are all about. The Y has no equal for providing programs for the development of kids from toddlers through the teen years.

I'd like to share a quote about kids from one of our great presidents, Theodore Roosevelt. He said: "Every kid has inside him an aching void for excitement. If we don't fill it with something that is exciting, interesting, and good for

him, he will fill it with something that is exciting, interesting, and which isn't good for him."

The Y has been supplying that excitement in a way that's
good for kids since it began in 1850. But it can't do it without
the help and support of people like you. Thank you for being
here.

WHY IT WORKS

Now imagine yourself in the audience hearing what you just said.
It's pretty good, isn't it? There had to be a beginning. The session
had to be opened. The audience needed to be connected to one
another and to the event. And you just did it. You've given the event
a common denominator and a perspective. Everyone present is now
"tuned in."

The very next thing you should do is give the audience an
overview of the agenda. Tell them what to expect. Include an indication
of how long the program will be. Now your listeners are comfortable.
They know the parameters. They will settle in.

YOUR SECOND RESPONSIBILITY—
TO INTRODUCE THE SPEAKERS

The next step is to get on with the program. Usually that means you
introduce the first speaker. Is there a right way to introduce a
speaker? You bet there is, and it begins with an understanding of
your responsibility as the go-between, the connecter of the audience
to the speaker.

It's similar to when you're hosting a party at your home and you
have guests who don't know one another. You feel an obligation to
introduce them, to tell each of them something about the other, so that
they will discover areas of common interest. You want to connect them
so that they can interact better. Once you have accomplished that, the
party becomes lively, the guests will talk more freely.

The same thing holds for the talk of introduction, though you
should go into a bit more detail, since the dialogue that takes place at
a party will be missing.

The word "introduce" comes from the Latin words *intro*, which
means inside, and *ducerem* which means to lead. When we introduce

a speaker properly, we lead the audience inside the speaker's world so that the audience is intrigued by the topic, impressed by the speaker's accomplishments, and excited to be present.

HOW TO ORGANIZE AN INTRODUCTION

Is there a simple way to organize such a talk? Of course there is. We call it the TEAS format. It was created by Charlie Windhorst, the cofounder of Communispond, twenty-five years ago, and has helped thousands of "introducers" perform this function flawlessly.

Here's how it works:

EMCEE FORMAT FOR INTRODUCTIONS

T Title of the speaker's talk; why it's important to this audience.

E Experience and Educational background of the speaker

A Anecdote about the speaker that:

- Reveals a human interest dimension of the speaker and/or
- Dramatizes the importance of the speaker's subject

S Speaker's name

Try to hold the speaker's name until last, even when the audience knows who the speaker is. It keeps the introduction cleaner and adds a sense of drama and a lift to the end of your intro.

To do this exceptionally, your first job is to interview the speaker and gather the necessary background information. You may have to work harder to get the anecdote. Sometimes the speaker is shy or "can't think of one." In that case, ask him or her for the name of a friend and phone that person to get the anecdote. Even if you encounter roadblocks, persist. It's worth it.

A SIMPLE LUNCHEON INTRO

J. Walter Thompson (JWT) was hosting a luncheon for the Ford Motor Company, its biggest account, to celebrate a new advertising campaign.

The luncheon would take place in the JWT executive dining area. About seventy people would be present, half Ford people, half JWT.

The JWT management supervisor, Glen Fortinberry, wanted the event to be special. He wanted a speaker who would appeal to this sports-oriented audience. So he arranged for Frank Gifford, the former all-pro Giants flankerback, to be a speaker. He also asked Charlie Windhorst to introduce Frank.

GATHERING INFORMATION

The first thing Charlie did was to call the New York Giants' office. He talked to Ray Walsh, the general manager, and told him that he was going to introduce Frank and that he wanted to tell the story of the great catch Frank made against the Steelers toward the end of his career, at Yankee Stadium.

Ray Walsh said, "I'll never forget that catch. We [the Giants] were in the race for the Eastern Divisional Championship of the NFL. We were tied. We had to beat the Steelers to get to the championship game. We were in the fourth quarter. It was third down with fourteen yards to go for a first. We were on our own forty-yard line. The quarterback was Y. A. Tittle. Gifford lined up left and ran a crossing pattern.

"Joe Walton, the tight end, was supposed to clear the area for Frank but was held up at the line of scrimmage. So Frank ran his pattern with two defenders on him. Y. A. was being rushed hard, but he held the ball as long as he could. He finally threw it out of desperation, and he threw it long. There was no way Frank could get to it . . . but he did. He dove, caught it with his fingertips, and tucked it in as he rolled on the ground. It was a first down. We went on to score, and we won the Divisional Championship. Frank's catch was the turning point."

Charlie took notes and was overjoyed because he knew he had a good anecdote! He also had prepared the other parts of the TEAS format.

NO SECRETS: TELL THE SPEAKER WHAT YOU'LL SAY

On the day of the luncheon, Charlie met with Frank Gifford and told him what he was going to say while introducing him. Not a bad idea. There's nothing worse than spouting some facts in your introduction and then having the speaker walk to the lectern and disclaim the truth of what you just said.

Let's look at the format for the talk of introduction as it applied to Charlie's intro of Frank Gifford. It follows the TEAS plan.

AN OUTLINE OF THE FRANK GIFFORD INTRODUCTION

Topic: "What it means to be a professional"

Charlie stated why that topic was important to this audience of Ford people: "Skill and professionalism separate the great ones from the not-so-greats in professional football; the same is true when creating great Ford advertising."

Experience and Education: Charlie provided facts about Gifford's professional background:

* Graduate of USC, where he was All-American

* NFL career 1952 to 1964

* Starred on both offense and defense during 1953 season

* All-NFL four years

* Seven Pro Bowls

* Pro Bowl selection in three different positions, as defensive back, halfback, and flanker

* Original team of broadcasters on *Monday Night Football*

* Covered the Olympics and other special events for ABC

Anecdote: Charlie told the story of Frank's catch against the Steelers. He made the point that the catch represented the epitome of professionalism.

Speaker's Name: Charlie simply said, "Ladies and gentlemen, I am happy to present our speaker today . . . (pause) . . . Frank Gifford."

Charlie had a little rubber football with him on the lectern, and as Frank walked to the lectern, Charlie tossed him the little football, which Frank caught and tossed back to him. Nice touch. Luckily, Frank caught the little football.

FRANK GIFFORD'S TRANSITION

Frank's opening remarks went something like this: "Thank you, Charlie, for the nice introduction. Actually, I'm not the one who deserves the credit for that play. Y. A. held his ground back there, looking death in the eye as two defensive linemen roared at him. After he threw the ball, he was almost annihilated by those tacklers. Any other quarterback would have thrown the ball away to avoid being hit so hard, and I wouldn't have had the chance to catch it.

"After the play, I congratulated Y. A. for holding the ball that long and then getting it to me. And he said, 'I wish I had thrown it to Del Shofner [a faster receiver] instead of you, Frank. Del would have been wide open, five yards in front of those defenders. It would have been an easy play, and I wouldn't have been hit by those linemen.' "

A GREAT INTRODUCTION IS ENJOYED BY ALL

That was Frank's transition into his talk. He was so self-effacing the audience loved him before he even started his prepared remarks. That's what a good anecdote can do for a speaker. It provides an opportunity for the speaker to gracefully transition from the introduction into his talk. But it's not just the speaker who benefits, the audience does, too. The entire affair rises to a new level if the introductions are done well.

After the luncheon was over, Frank sought Charlie out, thanked him again, and said, "Would you follow me around and introduce me whenever I speak?"

THE KEY, OF COURSE, IS THE ANECDOTE

If you can get a good anecdote, the speaker is "launched" with the audience. Charlie once introduced Ted Sorensen, a former speechwriter for President Kennedy, at one of those JWT events. Sorensen was a brilliant man who looked rather studious. In the introduction, Charlie said, (deliberately holding Ted's name until the end of the intro):

"Last week this man pitched a shut out and knocked in the winning run for his team in a slow pitch softball game in Central Park. And even after those heroics, he was much more elated by the team victory than by his own contributions. It shows what a team player this man is."

Notice how the story humanized Ted Sorensen. The audience could identify with him just a little bit more.

Sometimes it's difficult to get the necessary information, try though we might. We think we can get the material on the spot, and so we let it go until we have nowhere to turn for help. But we shouldn't excuse ourselves. Remember, a speaker cannot be as effective with a weak introduction. He cannot do it alone. You are there for a purpose. You are there to help make the event more meaningful, more enjoyable, than it could be without you.

SOMETIMES THE SETTING IS DIFFICULT

For many years I lived with my wife and family in Old Greenwich, Connecticut. One day in May, the organizer of the local Memorial Day parade asked me:

"Kevin, would you be willing to serve as the grand marshal of the parade? If you say 'yes,' here's what's involved:

"You would be part of the great parade, riding in the elevated back seat of the grand marshal's car as the parade weaves its way through town. Alongside of you would be our guest celebrity and featured speaker, Fred Furmark (not his real name), of TV fame. The parade will start at Todd's Point and work its way all the way down Sound Beach Avenue, ending at Memorial Rock.

"You and Fred will wave to the crowd during this journey. They will line the streets on both sides and be hanging off the train trestle bridge as you go under it. At Memorial Rock in Binney Park, you will introduce Fred. He will give his Memorial Day talk, and the parade will be over."

The whole thing sounded exciting to me, so I said, "Sure. I'll do it."

I knew how to do an introduction. It meant I'd have to get some information about the speaker, but I could get that from him as we inched our way along in the parade.

THE MEMORIAL DAY PARADE

Memorial Day came, and it wasn't long before I found myself in the back of the car with Fred Furmark on Shore Road in Old Greenwich, behind marching bands, baton twirlers, Veterans of American Wars, American Legion members, Girl Scouts, Daughters of the American

Revolution, the Fire Department, local officials, and just about any other organized group that wanted to walk or march from Todd's Point to Memorial Rock.

Fred and I were in the middle of all that. I told him I would be introducing him and asked him to tell me about his background. He said, "I've lived in this town for twenty years and they all know me here."

We were sitting high in the grand marshal's car, waving to the left, to the right, overhead. Wherever there were people waving, we waved back. It was fun. But I had a job to do. I needed information from my fellow "waver," and I was a little bit nervous about whether I was going to get it.

INTERVIEWING THE SPEAKER

So I said, "Fred, what is the topic of the talk you are going to give?"

He waved to the people standing in front of Sterling Watts's hardware store, and said, "I'm going to talk about patriotism."

I said: "I need a title for your talk."

Fred said, "How about 'What freedom means today'?"

I said, "I like it if you do."

At this point someone from the crowd yelled, "How are you doing, Fred?"

Fred answered, "I'm doing fine. I love being here with all of you."

We returned to our dialogue, still smiling, still waving. I said, "Could you tell me something about your background, your schooling?"

Fred said, "Why do you want to know about that?"

So I said, "I have to introduce you. I have to tell the people about you."

Fred said, "They all know me. I've lived in this town for twenty years."

I said, "Fred, please help me. I've got to introduce you, and I need some info on you. Would you help me?"

Little by little, Fred answered my questions and gave me what I needed. He never missed a wave. He smiled indefatigably. And a lot of the people did know him. I was really impressed with this fine man, but I sure struggled in getting enough information. I've changed a few details, but here is the outline of my introduction:

AN OUTLINE OF FRED'S INTRODUCTION

Topic: "What freedom means today"

Experience and education:
- Graduated from Fordham University
- Worked for his father as a law clerk for two years
- Went into broadcasting. Played Batman on radio for ten years
- Hosted *Deal and Cash In*
- Hosted *Winner Gets All*
- Hosted *Make a Million*
- Has hosted *The Truth Will Set You Free* for the last eight years
- Is considered the first game-show superstar
- Has had more exposure on daytime TV than any other TV personality

Anecdote: "Fred is a family man, with five children, four girls and a boy. Despite his fame and the demands on his time, the job he loves the most is that of superintendent of a Sunday school in our town of Greenwich. His deeply religious core shows itself when he bids adieu to both his Sunday school class and to the participants who perform on his show by saying, 'Good-bye, and may God be with you.'"

Speaker's Name: "Ladies and gentlemen, our celebrity Memorial Day speaker . . . (pause) . . . Fred Furmark."

Always announce the name with a rise of intonation and a burst of volume. The speaker's name is the culmination of your talk. If you have held the name until the end, the speaker will rise and walk toward you with outstretched hand as the audience applauds.

KEEP IT SHORT, THEN STEP OUT OF THE SPOTLIGHT
You might wonder how long the talk of introduction should be. The answer is—it should be short. Not longer than sixty seconds. Your job

is to sell the speaker to the audience, enhance his or her stature, tickle the audience's fancy, build their anticipation, and excite them about the speaker. All of that, but no more, in sixty seconds.

You are not the speaker. Don't be confused by that. You are there to prepare the way for the speaker, not compete with him or her. And, for heaven's sake, don't show off your knowledge about the speaker's subject. Here is an old speaker's lament:

> *Nothing makes me madder*
> *Than when the introducer's patter*
> *Is my subject matter*

YOUR THIRD RESPONSIBILITY— PRESENTING AWARDS

If you are program chair inside your company or organization, you will either present awards or direct others to do so. This is a special time. The award winners love it. The audience loves it. There are two scenarios to be dealt with; one is when you have a series of awards or acknowledgments, and the other is when you are presenting the coveted top awards.

EXAMPLES OF A SERIES OF AWARDS

- Members of a team who worked together
- People who reached new sales "highs"
- Top producers in different categories
- People who helped make an event successful
- Those who made quota
- Extraordinary accomplishment

When you are delivering an award, make sure you clearly state what the accomplishment was. Dramatize it. Make it sound important. Be enthusiastic. Be happy. Be upbeat. Be impressed.

Hold the name until last. Announce it with gusto. Smile at each recipient. Shake their hands. Show how delighted you are. Remember that your speech—what you say and how you say it—is a massive part of the award. You create the aura. You create the magnitude. You create the sense of triumph. If you do it well, the award winners will revel in their moment. Potential recipients will be motivated to strive for the same recognition in the future. The audience will be impressed. The event will be a success. And you will be responsible for that success.

MAKE SURE YOU PRONOUNCE THE NAMES CORRECTLY

The best way to sidestep this common error is to practice pronouncing the names. The best time to botch a name is in private. There are no penalty points for that, but if you do it out loud to the audience, that's the one thing they will remember—and they will think you're a jerk. That's not fair, but that's the way it is. As Dale Carnegie once said, "Remember, a man's name is, to him, the sweetest and most important sound in any language."

Don't ever lose sight of the fact that these people are being singled out for recognition. It's a marvelous moment, each time—for them. If you are bored with it, or it comes off as dull or perfunctory, you have failed. You lose personal stature with all those present. So, keep your enthusiasm at a high level from beginning to end, no matter how long and drawn-out the ceremony may become. Even if it sometimes seems to you that you are going on forever, remember that it is the first time and the only time for each person being recognized.

THE COVETED TOP AWARDS

Ideally there should be but one of these, just as there is only one Congressional Medal of Honor. But it's easy to make a case for two. Is there an absolute limit to how many top awards there can be? Yes. The outside limit is three. Beyond that, there is no exclusivity. The value is tarnished.

In many companies, the top award gets its name from some event in the company's history. Let me give you an example. At Communispond, the top honor you can receive is the Jack Sloan Broken Pick Award.

THE STORY BEHIND THE BROKEN PICK AWARD

Jack Sloan was a great old-timer who joined Communispond as a salesman at the age of sixty-five and worked for us for eight years. He was marvelously successful because he worked hard and he worked smart. Our vice president of sales, Ted Fuller, was so impressed with his work ethic that he used Jack as an example at one of our sales meetings saying, "You never have to wonder where Jack is. If you can't find him in the office, it's because he's at a client somewhere, breaking his pick (as in digging a hole with a pickax), trying to make a sale."

And so was born the Broken Pick Award. It goes to the person who best demonstrates that they "went the extra mile," "broke their pick," to make the sale. The award, given once a year, is a plaque with the broken pickax symbol on it. It's the apex, the epitome of recognition. You might think a broken pick isn't too glamorous. But that's where tradition and company culture come in. No award is more meaningful or more coveted at Communispond.

When presenting a coveted top award, do so with much excitement and joy. Show that you are thrilled to be a part of this great moment and to be sharing it with everyone in the room. Follow these five simple steps:

1. Tell the story and the philosophy of the award.

2. Lay out the success record and accomplishments of the recipient.

3. Explain how the accomplishments demonstrate the philosophy.

4. Hold the name until last even though they know who it is.

5. Say the name with gusto.

KEY LEARNINGS FOR HOW TO EMCEE A MEETING, INTRODUCE A SPEAKER, AND PRESENT AWARDS

Do:

- Consider yourself honored if you are asked to be a program chair. It's a showcase for you. It will do more for your stature and visibility in your company than six months of normal work.

- Use the TEAS formula when introducing a speaker. It's simple and it works. The introduction will be livelier and the speaker better launched.

- Make sure you get a good anecdote; it makes your introduction special. It also sets up the speaker, and the audience loves it.

- Hold the name for last when you introduce a speaker or present an award. It helps build anticipation. The audience will applaud more enthusiastically.
- Punch the name with gusto when you announce the speaker or the award winner's name.

Don't:

- Use the person's name ten or fifteen times in the course of the introduction. This strips all drama from the ending.
- Talk too long. You are the preface, not the book.
- Try to steal the show by being a comedian or by seeking undue attention. Not your job. There's a place in heaven for a good emcee. Most comedians never get there.

16

HOW TO DELIVER
A TALK TO INSPIRE

RECENTLY, **I** HAD A COACHING SESSION with a divisional
president of a Fortune 500 company. The first thing I did
was ask her how she would like to be perceived by an
audience. I told her to select ten characteristics that
would be an appropriate ending to the sentence, "I'd like
an audience to see me as . . ."
Here's what she wrote:

Enthusiastic

Persuasive

Credible

Honest

Confident

Exciting

Natural

Inspiring

Sincere

Knowledgeable

That was the order. Then I asked her to pick her top four. Here's how she listed them:

Honest

Knowledgeable

Inspiring

Sincere

I asked, "Why those four?" She said, "I want people to see me as being transparently open with them—no secrets. That's honest. And I want them to believe me and believe in me, to see me as a knowledgeable expert, and to respect me. And I'd like to be seen as sincere and inspiring."

"Very good," I said. "Now the tough decision. Which of these would you select if you could only choose one?"

"Oh, to be inspiring," she said. "If you are able to do that, the audience loves you. That's the ultimate dream of any speaker! But very few ever accomplish it." I asked her when she might see herself giving an inspirational talk. "Often when I give a state-of-the-business update to my department, I feel the need to be inspirational," she said. "To show them that their world will get better if we just reach a little more, and try a little harder. That's an example. Another is whenever I address the sales force. The sales people always need a lift. The sales manager beats on them all the time. He doesn't inspire; he manages, he persuades, he bribes them with incentives. When I come in, I'm management. What I try to do is create a bigger picture for them, a loftier vision. I want to lift their sights, to inspire them. That's what they need."

LEARNING BY EXAMPLE: GREAT INSPIRATIONAL TALKS

It is true that giving a talk to inspire is challenging. But it is a skill that can be learned. The word "inspire" comes from the Latin *inspirae*, which means "to breathe life into." It enables you, the speaker, to breathe life into your talk and into your audience. That is why the talk to inspire is so riveting. It is why you, the speaker, come away looking so strong.

Let's examine a few great inspirational talks from history, recognizing that the world's stage belonged to those great people at those moments. You and I don't have that stage, but we do have our own settings, whatever they may be. We can learn from the masters, draw some principles from them, and show how those same principles, with some adaptation, can work for us.

PATRICK HENRY

Consider the American Patrick Henry in March of 1775. The tensions between the colonists and the British had escalated. War, even revolution, was openly discussed. Much preparation was underway, but Virginia, the largest colony, had not committed itself. A meeting of its delegates was held in Richmond. Patrick Henry proffered a number of resolutions. His purpose was to inspire these delegates to take the big step. They should no longer see themselves as independent farmers, husbands, tradesmen, private citizens, but as fellow countrymen, seeking freedom. Patrick Henry proposed to put the colony of Virginia "into a posture of defense . . . embodying, arming, and disciplining such a number of men as may be sufficient for that purpose." It was a commitment to revolution.

Here are the last two paragraphs of his historic speech:

> The battle, sir, is not to the strong alone; it is to the vigilant, the active, the brave. Besides, sir, we have no election. If we were base enough to desire it, it is now too late to retire from the contest. There is no retreat but in submission and slavery! Our chains are forged! Their clanking may be heard on the plains of Boston! The war is inevitable—and let it come! I repeat it, sir, let it come!
>
> It is in vain, sir, to extenuate the matter. Gentlemen may cry, "Peace! Peace!"—but there is no peace. The war is

actually begun! The next gale that sweeps from the north
will bring to our ears the clash of resounding arms! Our
brethren are already in the field! Why stand we here idle!
What is it that gentlemen wish? What should they have?
Is life so dear, or peace so sweet, as to be purchased at
the price of chains and slavery? Forbid it, Almighty God!
I know not what course others may take; but as for me, give
me liberty, or give me death!

He spoke without a script and his speech was effective. At its conclusion a vote was taken, and the resolutions passed by a narrow
margin. Virginia had thereby joined in the American Revolution.

Note how Patrick Henry lifted his audience beyond where they
could go by themselves. The appeal was to a higher goal for his listeners—freedom versus slavery. He showed he was committed to the
cause he was espousing. He rallied them; he inspired them.

WINSTON CHURCHILL

Here is a Winston Churchill speech from May 13, 1940. Sir Winston
had just been appointed British Prime Minister the Friday before. In
that short time, he had formed a war cabinet made up of five members
that he described as "representing, with the Labour, opposition, and
Liberals, the unity of the nation." England was the prime target of
Hitler's war machine, and the very survival of the country was in
doubt. The speech was relatively short. At its end, Sir Winston said, "I
take up my task in buoyancy and hope . . . Come then, let us go forward
together with our united strength."

But just before that, he said these immortal words:

I say to the House as I said to ministers who have joined
this government, I have nothing to offer but blood, toil,
tears and sweat. We have before us an ordeal of the most
grievous kind. We have before us many, many months of
struggle and suffering.

You ask, what is our policy? I say it is to wage war by
land, sea, and air. War with all our might and with all the
strength God has given us, and to wage war against a monstrous tyranny never surpassed in the dark and lamentable
catalogue of human crime. That is our policy.

You ask, what is our aim? I can answer in one word. It is
victory. Victory at all costs—Victory in spite of all terrors—
Victory, however long and hard the road may be, for without
victory there is no survival.

Note that Churchill took his listeners on a mental and emotional journey created by his words and feelings: "ordeal of the most grievous
kind," "months of struggle and suffering," "war against a monstrous
tyranny," "victory in spite of all terrors." There was no way his audience could remain unmoved. With his inspirational speech he galva-
nized their thoughts and their emotions, so that they went "forward
together with [their] united strength."

PRESIDENT JOHN F. KENNEDY
On January 20, 1961, John Fitzgerald Kennedy delivered his inaugu-
ral address. He was the youngest U.S. president ever and had won the
presidency by the narrowest margin ever—110,000 popular votes. The
day was cold, twenty-two degrees. He wore no overcoat and no hat.

Carl Sandburg, the poet, later said of that address ". . . around
nearly every sentence . . . could be written a thesis, so packed it is with
implications."

Here are excerpts from that talk:

We observe today not a victory of party but a celebration of freedom, symbolizing an end as well as a beginning,
signifying renewal as well as change . . .

Let the word go forth from this time and place, to friend
and foe alike, that the torch has been passed to a new generation of Americans, born in this century, tempered by war,
disciplined by a hard and bitter peace, proud of our ancient
heritage, and unwilling to witness or permit the slow undo-
ing of these human rights to which this nation has always
been committed, and to which we are committed today at
home and around the world.

Let every nation know, whether it wishes us well or ill,
that we shall pay any price, bear any burden, meet any
hardship, support any friend, oppose any foe, to assure the
survival and the success of liberty. This much we pledge—
and more . . .

And so, my fellow Americans, ask not what your country can do for you; ask what you can do for your country. My fellow citizens of the world, ask not what America will do for you, but what together we can do for the freedom of man.

At the conclusion of that talk our nation came together behind John F. Kennedy. He had created a vision of the future that we all aspired to. His vision, but now ours, too. He asked for our participation to make that vision a reality. He lifted us out of ourselves and took us with him, through his talk, to a better world. That is what a great talk to inspire can do.

Each of these examples is among the finest inspirational talks of all time. Let's identify the common elements and then see how we might use them.

1. The grandeur of the vision. (Example: "freedom of citizens versus slavery," Patrick Henry)

2. The total commitment of the speaker. (Example: "I have nothing to offer but blood, toil, tears and sweat," Winston Churchill)

3. How the speaker reaches for our participation. (Example: "Ask not what your country can do for you . . . ," John F. Kennedy)

4. An appeal to nobler motives. (Example: "Victory, however long and hard the road may be, because without victory there is no survival," Winston Churchill)

5. How the audience is uplifted. (Example: " . . . ask what together we can do for the freedom of man," John F. Kennedy)

CREATING YOUR OWN INSPIRING MESSAGE

But let's step back. How do we, you and I, put together a talk to inspire? We are not the leaders of nations or the fomenters of revolution. We usually don't have a cataclysmic world event as a backdrop. Instead, we have a variety of business situations where we might want to inspire, such as a sales meeting, motivating a team on a new project, a departmental meeting, a midyear update, an annual meeting, a meeting requesting an additional budget allocation, and so on. There are many opportunities, and the ability to inspire a group is never out of style.

Where do we find the material for such a talk? We reach into our own life experience and find stories that were "moving" to us as we lived through them, and tell them in a way that moves our audience. There has to be a message or lesson that flows from the story, and it has to be pertinent to that audience at that time. That's what we will explore now.

We'll establish principles, analyze two examples, and see how it all fits together.

PRINCIPLES FOR AN INSPIRATIONAL TALK

1. Begin with a moving story.

2. Re-create and relive the story.

3. Show and share your feelings.

4. End with a lesson learned.

---

1. Begin with a moving story. This can be an incident out of your life that had a profound emotional impact on you, or a profound incident from someone else's life that you know so well and feel so deeply that you can tell it as though you were there.

2. Create and relive the story. We've talked about the impact of a story in other chapters. Here, the story is more important because the stakes are so much higher. Re-create, relive the story with words, gestures and energy so that the audience sees what you saw, hears what you heard, feels what you felt, lives through the experience the way you did.

3. Show your feelings. Share your feelings. Give totally of yourself. Don't hold back. Patrick Henry, Winston Churchill, and John Kennedy each showed their most heartfelt emotions and convictions in the speeches they gave.

4. End with the message or the lesson learned. If your goal is to inspire people to greater efforts, be sure your final words are uplifting. Ensure that the audience will be moved to action.

EXAMPLE ONE: A TALE OF TWO LITTLE GIRLS

Many years ago I heard a talk that lifted me out of myself and stayed with me for a lifetime. The speaker was a woman named Marie DeMarco (not her real name). She was speaking to a Dale Carnegie class of about forty people. She told a simple story about her two little girls. Her purpose, which all the audience understood, was to deliver an inspirational talk. She told the story with profound feeling, and, indeed, she inspired us all.

THE STORY

Begin at a point in time. It is important to orient the audience. The two main elements of that orientation are time and place:

> Last Saturday night, December third, my husband and I had a party at our house. We invited six couples for six o'clock cocktails to be followed by dinner at seven.

Next, set the stage. Introduce the people who are at the core of the story. Tell us enough of what is coming up so that our anticipation builds. When you do this, remember that detail is important, but not extraneous detail. It should be kept tight. Notice how the detail in this story makes the scene and the people more real:

> We have two daughters: Kristen is seven years old, and Kelly is four. I dressed them up for the party: White taffeta dresses, blue ribbons in their hair, white socks, and patent leather shoes. I even took them to the beauty parlor to have their hair done. It was the first time either of them had been to a beauty parlor. They loved it and felt so special. I told my girls that the whole family had a responsibility to make sure the party went well. I would serve the food. Daddy would fix the cocktails. And they had a job, too. They would join Mommy in answering the door when the bell rang. Mommy would introduce them to the guests, and then they would take the guests' coats upstairs and put them on the bed in the second bedroom.

My goodness, they were excited! They were all dressed up. They were beautiful. And they were playing an important role at the party.

Now, describe what happened.

The guests arrived. I introduced my two daughters to each of them. The adults were gracious and kind and said how lucky we parents were to have such good kids who would help with the coats.

Each of the guests (all twelve or so it seemed) made a particular fuss over Kelly, the younger one, admiring her dress, her hair, her pert little nose, her smile. They said she was a remarkable girl to be carrying coats upstairs at her age.

I thought to myself that we adults tend to make a big "to do" over the younger one because she's the one who seems more vulnerable. We do it with the best of intentions.

But we seldom think of how it might affect the other child. I was a little worried that Kristen would feel she was being outshined. I looked at her from time to time, and she wasn't smiling as Kelly was. But the party went on, and I put it out of my mind.

An hour went by. I was about to serve dinner, but I was vaguely disturbed that Kristen, my seven-year-old, wasn't puttering around the kitchen with her sister. I realized she had been missing for about twenty minutes. I went upstairs to see where she was. I checked her room. I checked the room with the coats. Then I opened the closed door of the master bedroom and there she was, standing in front of the full-length mirror, pirouetting, looking at herself. She had tear tracks on her face. She had been crying.

I said, "What are you doing, my dear?"

She turned to me with that empty, sad expression and said, "Mommy, why don't people like me the way they like my sister? Is it because I'm not pretty? Is that why they don't say nice things about me as much?"

Then she ran to me, put her arms around my legs, and burst into tears. She was crushed, and I was soon hurting as much as she was. I couldn't stand seeing my seven-year-old daughter so devastated. I tried to explain. We talked for fifteen minutes, and I held her. I kissed her. I hugged her. Then I had to go back downstairs to my guests. But I vowed to myself that I would never make the same mistake when dealing with other people's children.

THE MESSAGE

The message comes at the end of the talk. It should be short and crisp. A good inspirational message should flow naturally out of the story. It has no real value in itself. Its value comes from the story that precedes it; we don't preach. We don't have to turn it into an action step, though we can if the situation demands it. The message is the lesson we learned.

The objective of your talk should be to lift the audience to a new level of understanding, to inspire them with the story so that their lives will be enlarged and changed by your experience.

Now, whenever I visit a friend's home I make it a point to speak to the older child first, ask what she is doing in school, praise her, or dote on her. When I leave the house, I want that older child to feel how truly special he or she is.

I do this because I know the younger ones will get their share of attention. And I know, just as surely, the older ones won't. And we should make a point to give it to them, not by neglecting the little ones but by deliberately giving the older ones more than their full share.

Notice how you the reader are moved by the story. The people seem real. You can identify with them. It is a simple story, which appeals to your nobler motives and changes your perspective from that moment on.

EXAMPLE TWO: BREAKING THE SOUND BARRIER

I was asked to speak at a dinner honoring 120 salespeople for having achieved Gold Circle status as top sales producers for the company.

The purpose of my talk was to demonstrate that management was aware of the extraordinary effort it took to produce those results. I was also told that my talk should lift the spirit of the sales force and inspire them to go forward and do it again.

Here is the ending of that talk, the inspirational part:

> When Mike introduced me, he mentioned that I was a former Navy pilot. I'd like to share a story that you can relate to, because it's all about overcoming obstacles. And you wouldn't be sitting here if you had let obstacles overcome you.

THE STORY

Begin at a point in time and place. The audience must be able to orient themselves or we lose them in the narrative.

> When I was twenty-one years old, I enlisted in the Navy (people did that in my day because it was better than being drafted). Shortly after that I went to naval flight school and, a year-and-a-half later, received my wings and became a naval aviator.
>
> Next step was to be assigned to a squadron in Oceana, Virginia. In a matter of days I was flying the hottest Navy jet there was at the time—the F/U-3 Cutlass. I was elated. The Cutlass was one of the first Navy planes to be able to break the sound barrier.

Now we set the stage. Notice in the next paragraphs, how the detail fuels anticipation for what might happen later. It draws the audience into the story by educating them a little bit and preparing them to better understand the outcome or lesson.

> But that wasn't as easy as it sounds. In those days, planes didn't have the power or the airframe to break the sound barrier flying straight and level. Instead, the pilot had to get as much altitude as he could, then dive straight down, breaking through the sound barrier while diving toward the earth.

Nonetheless, I couldn't wait. I had only been with the squadron a short time when I asked for the opportunity to go supersonic. First I had to go through a lengthy briefing, read manuals, and sign all sorts of forms.

The briefing was really interesting. We had only one pilot, our executive officer, Commander Jim Ferris, who had already broken the sound barrier, so he was the official briefer. During that briefing, he told me that just before going through Mach 1 (the speed of sound), at about Mach .97, the plane would start buffeting. Then as the speed inched closer to Mach 1, the buffeting would get so bad that I would be tempted to give up and abort the mission. (Each of you in this room has been in a similar position when the buyer puts up obstacles that seemed insurmountable.)

Then Jim put his hands on my shoulders and said, "Kevin, you've got to commit yourself to getting the thing done, or you'll back off at the last moment. You've got to close the exit doors in your mind or you'll fail—because it's scary, believe me."

Then he said, "On the other hand, if you've got the guts and you do it, you'll feel like a million bucks. You'll be one of the exclusive few." So I said to him, with all of the bravado of a twenty-two-year old, "Don't worry about me backing off, Jim, I'll stay with it."

Now describe the action. Detail is important but notice how it's not drawn out:

The next day, Saturday, was my day. I took off at 9:30 A.M., climbed to 47,500 feet, and headed for Dismal Swamp, a huge uninhabited tract of land in Virginia. In the center of the swamp is a lake, almost perfectly round, named Lake Drummond.

Then came the moment of truth. I was over the lake, full throttle, both afterburners on. I followed the procedure. I turned the plane on its back and pulled the nose gently through to the vertical. I was pointed directly at Lake Drummond. The Mach gage

Figure 16–1. What breaking the sound barrier looks like. (Photo courtesy of authors.)

was rising. I saw .93, then .95, then .97. The buffeting began, not bad at first, then more and more.

It was so violent my eyes were slightly out of focus. I couldn't see clearly. My helmeted head bounced off the side of the canopy from one side to the other. Lake Drummond was coming up to meet me and coming fast.

I was at .99 and really scared. I wanted to abort. And I think I would have—except that Jim's words about being committed were ever present in my mind, and I knew I couldn't face him if I backed off.

So I gritted my teeth and held on.

Then, suddenly, it was perfectly smooth. I had broken through the sound barrier! The gage said 1.0, then a little more.

"I did it! I did it!" I screamed to myself.

Then, just as suddenly, I realized that I couldn't bask in that glory for long because that lake was getting bigger and bigger. I'd better change the direction my plane was headed in, or within a few seconds I'd be a wet, dead naval aviator, and none of this would matter very much.

So I pulled off the throttles and began pulling back the nose of the aircraft. It was over. I had made it. I had broken the sound barrier.

THE MESSAGE

If you examine the story up to this point, you can almost feel that the audience needs a "wrap up" or an answer to the query, "So what does that mean?" or "How does that affect me?" That's what the speaker must do now. But remember that an inspirational message must flow out of the story. It's not an action step, as in a talk to persuade. It is simply a natural conclusion emanating from the story:

That was a great moment in my life, and I loved it, but I learned a lesson from that experience that I'd like to share with you. Let me restate it as Commander Ferris said it:

"You've got to commit yourself to getting the thing done."

"You've got to close the exit doors in your mind or you'll fail."

And when you think about it, those words apply just as much to you as they did to me. You broke the sound barrier. You pushed beyond quota. You overcame obstacles. You wouldn't be defeated. You closed the exit doors in your mind. You got the job done. That's why we are all here tonight for this special celebration.

So tonight I salute you, and your management salutes you. You have achieved Gold Circle status. You are among the special few. My congratulations!

In both of the examples, you can feel how the audience enters into the story and relates the events to their individual lives. The stories deal with essential human values (inspirational talks always do).

They appeal to the nobler motives of the people in attendance. The audience is uplifted.

DELIVERY: SHOW YOUR EMOTIONS

The talk to inspire is all about sharing. You are sharing an experience that profoundly affected you. The impact on the audience depends on you showing its impact on you. As a Roman poet once said:

> *If you would draw tears from another's eyes,*
> *yourself the signs of grief must show.*

That means you must show your feelings to be effective. If there is anguish, you must show anguish. If there is anger, you must show anger. If joy, then joy. The audience needs to see how you feel so that they can experience the same emotion. There are no short cuts. Wordy explanations won't do it. Emotion will.

A LAST WORD

Most speakers never attempt to give an inspirational talk. There is a "sound barrier" that stands in their way. They are willing to give a talk to inform or to persuade or to convince. But the thought of being inspirational frightens them. They are afraid to extend themselves into an emotional area. Afraid they won't get it right, that they are taking a chance; afraid that they will look foolish if they show their feelings. Afraid that the talk will expose their vulnerability, their soft side, their humanity.

Indeed, it does. And therein lies its power and its magic.

Where does the talk to inspire fit in your repertoire as a speaker? It's the top of the ladder, the peak of the mountain. It demonstrates that you have broken through as a speaker. You have gone where few speakers dare to go.

And you will be remembered for it. You will breathe life into an audience. You will change the way people look at the world. You will make a difference in their lives. You will become one of the exclusive few. It will take a commitment on your part. You'll have to "close the exit doors in your mind" to achieve it.

But once you give a successful inspirational talk, you'll feel on top of the world. So will the audience. And all will know that you shared an important moment together.

KEY LEARNINGS FOR DELIVERING
A TALK TO INSPIRE

Do:

* Select a story that had great emotional impact on you.
* Make sure the story has an implied message that is right for the audience.
* Tell it well, with strong emotion. Pull out all the stops.
* End with an uplifting "lesson learned."

Don't:

* Drag out the story. Short is better than long.
* Try to explain a lot. Let the story do the work.
* Think you can be detached and be successful. You have to bleed up there. But it will be worth it.

INDEX

ABOUT THE AUTHORS

KEVIN DALEY has spent the last forty years helping people develop their communications skills. In 1969 he founded Communispond Inc., which has since trained over 450,000 executives worldwide. Kevin also worked in the advertising industry and is a former U.S. Navy jet pilot. He now lives with his wife, Ann, in Connecticut. His first book, *Socratic Selling: How to Ask the Questions That Get the Sale,* was published with Emmett Wolfe in 1996.

LAURA DALEY-CARAVELLA has eighteen years experience in the design and delivery of executive skill development programs. Additionally Laura worked for Citibank for seven years. She lives in Connecticut with her husband, David, and two children, Ryan and Kelly.